"The Lord is leading us into a season to go deeper—deeper in understanding, deeper in confrontation. *Authority to Tread* is a practical guide to warfare that reveals the full scope of understanding the enemy in the atmosphere around you, in the land you walk on and in the societal structures that affect the way we live. Rebecca fully reveals how to get your feet planted firmly over the enemy's plan in your region."

Dr. Chuck D. Pierce, president, Glory of Zion International, Inc.; vice president, Global Harvest Ministries

"I have served alongside Becca in the trenches on a prayer journey to Nepal just short of the foot of Mount Everest in 1997. She is a serious student and practitioner of all three levels of spiritual warfare, and I am delighted that she has now become an excellent teacher of this highly specialized subject, drawing on her solid, extensive experience. What a delight for me personally to see the baton of strategic-level spiritual warfare passed into such capable hands of the next generation!"

Doris Wagner, executive vice president, Global Harvest Ministries

"*Authority to Tread* will strengthen your faith to achieve great things for God. Having mentored Becca, I can say she is humble, gentle, teachable, but a fierce warrior for the issues that are on God's heart. Her book reflects with honesty the joy of victory as well as the lessons of failure. Becca is a seasoned intercessor and unfolds the strategies of warfare with clarity and skill. I highly recommend this easy-reading and faith-building book."

Alice Smith, executive director, U.S. Prayer Center

"*Authority to Tread* is not another complex theological treatise on spiritual warfare and spiritual mapping. Not at all! It is a wonderfully clear, concise and, best of all, practical guide for every praying Christian written by an internationally experienced practitioner. Thanks, Becca!"

Eddie Smith, president, U.S. Prayer Center

"I love Becca Greenwood's approach to spiritual warfare: marriages on the brink of divorce are restored; a rock concert overtly propagating Satanism is thwarted; 'gentlemen's clubs' are shut down and their clientele inexplicably flee the premises; thousands of Christians across the globe are led in informed, targeted spiritual warfare with a view to establishing God's Kingdom rule.

"I assure you, this is not the stuff of Sunday-school classes. Becca treats us to provocative insight into the believer's authority to reorder situations and circumstances through dynamic intercession and powerful spiritual warfare.

"Most of all, I like this book because Becca reminds us so eloquently of Jesus' words in Matthew 11:12: 'From the days of John the Baptist until now, the Kingdom of heaven suffers violence, and *strong men and women who propagate the dynamic of God's reign are forcefully advancing it*' (italicized portion paraphrased from the original Greek translation)."

Joseph Thompson, president, Light the Nations Ministries; coeditor, *Out of Africa*; author, *I'm a Christian, So How Can I Have Demons?*

"*Authority to Tread* encourages the reader to enlarge a personal prayer perspective to a global vision and to press forward into new vistas in partnership with the Lord. Rebecca Greenwood relates dynamic, real-life experiences in intercession, releasing faith and excitement in the power of prayer. This book will enrich your life!"

Lora Allison, president, Celebration International Ministries; author, *Skinned Alive? The Importance of Covering*

AUTHORITY TO
TREAD

A PRACTICAL GUIDE
FOR STRATEGIC-LEVEL
SPIRITUAL WARFARE

REBECCA
GREENWOOD

Chosen
Grand Rapids, Michigan

© 2005 by Rebecca Greenwood

Published by Chosen Books
A division of Baker Publishing Group
P.O. Box 6287, Grand Rapids, MI 49516-6287
www.chosenbooks.com

Third printing, October 2006

Printed in the United States of America

Library of Congress Cataloging-in-Publication Data
Greenwood, Rebecca, 1967–
    Authority to tread : a practical guide for strategic-level spiritual warfare / Rebecca Greenwood.
        p.   cm.
    Includes bibliographical references and index.
    ISBN 10: 0-8007-9387-0 (pbk.)
    ISBN 978-0-8007-9387-6 (pbk.)
    1. Spiritual warfare. I. Title.
    BV4509.5.G68 2005
    235'.4—dc22   2004016907

To my wonderful husband, best friend and partner in ministry, Greg.
Thank you for believing in me and encouraging me in the call of the Lord on my life. I love you.

Contents

5. Exposing Hidden Truths   81

Knowing the facts equips intercessors to hit the bull's eye while engaging in warfare prayer.

6. Spiritual Mapping   89

Successful spiritual warfare is dependent on the indispensable tool of spiritual mapping—putting all the information together and laying out the battle plans.

7. Preparing for Battle   101

Your mission is clear. Now is the time for all the practical considerations of praying "on location" as well as a personal spiritual inventory.

8. Advancing into Battle   119

The time has come to advance! Now the battle begins. Effective on-site prayer brings breakthrough.

9. Counterattack   135

When a prayer team begins to advance in its God-given authority and wage war against the schemes of the enemy, it will face counterattack. Learn how to stand successfully against these assaults.

10. Breakthrough!   143

When successful strategic-level warfare has occurred, reports of breakthrough in the region will begin to emerge.

Foreword

THE DAY JOHN baptized Jesus in the Jordan River was the day of an invasion so great that, by comparison, it could make D-Day of World War II seem like a mere video game. From that day on, Jesus and His disciples began preaching the Gospel of the Kingdom of God.

A "kingdom," by definition, has a government headed up by a king. Jesus was the invading King. The kingdom He was invading also had a government, and its king was Satan. For thousands of years after the time of Adam and Eve, the human population of the whole world, with a few exceptions such as the people of God in Israel, was under the evil control of the prince of the power of the air. Practically speaking Satan could do anything he wanted to the peoples of the earth. And what he did was not good.

Things changed radically when God sent His Son. From the time of Jesus until now, the war has been hot and it is getting hotter. The Kingdom of God has been advancing as it always has advanced—namely, by force (see Matthew 11:12). Satan's fury continues to swell because he knows his time is shorter than it ever has been.

Jesus started the war, and He will conclude it when He returns. But meanwhile He is not with us personally; He is at the right hand of the Father making intercession for those of us who make up His Church. He has delegated His Church to continue the war by spreading the Gospel of the Kingdom to all the peoples of earth. By itself the Church would not have the power to confront the forces of Satan. So when Jesus went to the Father, He sent the Holy Spirit who, from that point on, has provided divine power to all who will receive it. Jesus' presence with us—He said, "Lo, I am with you always"—now comes through the third Person of the Trinity.

Jesus did not leave the earth, however, without delegating His authority to those of us who follow Him as Lord. He told His disciples that they would receive power when the Holy Spirit came upon them. He gave them a command to make disciples of all nations. He authorized them to use His name and to move against the enemy in His kingly authority.

What does this mean? It means that the war to continue pushing Satan and his wicked forces back by the Gospel of the Kingdom of God is now in the hands of the Church, the people of God. In other words, we as the Church are at war!

What, then, do we do? How do we go about fighting this war? What are the marching orders? If we have authority, how much do we have? How can we discern the battle plan of the enemy? What are the risks? Do all go to war or do some stay by the stuff? Who are the generals in the army of God? How do we know if we are winning or losing? Does God provide us with new weapons of warfare? How is the Church trained for battle?

In this book Rebecca Greenwood—her friends know her as "Becca"—addresses these questions and many more head on. Becca is superbly qualified to do so because she brings to the table the unusual qualities of an intercessor who is both right-brained and left-brained. She hears from God, she flows in the Spirit, she is known to explode with fury at the enemy, but at the same time she is quietly analyzing what is going on at any given moment and planning strategy for the next move. Many intercessors do their work in the prayer closet and, with the door closed, have a powerful ministry. Becca spends much time in the closet as well, but she also battles on the front lines. As an experienced "eagle of God," she has found herself on spiritual battlefields in such diverse locations as Mount Everest in Nepal; St. Petersburg, Russia; Santiago de Compostela, Spain; and many other places.

I mention this to affirm that the author of *Authority to Tread* is no novice, and she has the battle scars to prove it. She is convinced that the war is not over. The 1990s saw an explosion of literature designed to equip the Body of Christ for sustained warfare, and this book picks up the torch for the 2000s. We know more now than we knew then, and Becca keeps us up-to-date. God continues to give new revelation. The enemy has his back to the wall. This is no time to yield to the Christian antiwar movement. Becca pushes us forward powerfully from strength to strength, building on the advantage we have gained over the past ten or fifteen years.

Authority to Tread is crammed with analysis, insight and information. Added to that come the heart-stirring inspiration and understanding of Rebecca Greenwood's personal experiences in wrestling with principalities and powers and spiritual hosts of wickedness in heavenly places.

You may have read and digested some of the earlier books on strategic-level spiritual warfare. If so, you can now look forward to another sumptuous feast and to being energized with the vital spiritual nourishment you need in order to move ahead into God's next season for your life.

C. Peter Wagner
Colorado Springs, Colorado

Acknowledgments

THIS BOOK WOULD not have been possible without the help, love, confirmation and mentoring of many people who have tremendously blessed my life. First I want to say thank you to my wonderful husband, Greg, who has tirelessly encouraged, loved and provided for me through the writing of this book. Thank you for the weekends of taking care of the girls, doing the laundry, cleaning the house and most of all pressing and encouraging me to complete this book. Thank you for believing in me and releasing me to the nations to pray. You complete me. You are the best! I love you.

Next I want to thank my three beautiful daughters, Kendall, Rebecca and Katie, for putting up with a mother who has spent long hours writing and typing at the computer over the past year and a half. You are precious!

To my parents, Ronnie and Mary Long, you are awesome! Thank you for loving, supporting and believing in me. Thank you for all the sacrifices you have made throughout my life to help me achieve my dreams. You have always given 100 percent as parents and taught me how to achieve in all areas of life. I have always felt loved and cherished by both of you. You have blessed me and my children with a righteous inheritance. No words can express my love for both of you.

To my wonderful in-laws, Jack and Pam Greenwood, I want to say thank you. You have accepted me and loved me as your own. Thank you for the love, encouragement and spiritual counsel you have always given me. I love you both.

I could not write this book without expressing my sincere love and gratitude to Eddie and Alice Smith. The two of you took Greg and me under your wing and poured yourselves into our lives. Thank you for the mentoring, love, wisdom, support and friendship. I will always cherish our relationship. Thank you for passing down to the next generation the precious anointing the Lord has placed on each of you. I love you.

To Lora Allison, what do I say? Thank you for being my friend. You gave me the strength and hope to move forward when I felt I could not. Your love and support have enabled me to press forward and to flow in the gifts that the Lord has given me. You are a precious, loving, prophetic voice to the Body of Christ. Thank you for loving and believing in me.

Peg Howerton, I want to say thank you from the bottom of my heart for the many hours of helping me polish numerous portions of this book. You are a precious servant of God and I pray tremendous blessing over you and John. I could not have done this without you. May the Lord bless you abundantly!

To Peter and Doris Wagner, thank you for your encouragement and the tremendous opportunity to work for Global Harvest Ministries. Thank you for the example that you walk before the Body of Christ and your lifetime of total commitment to the Lord and the call He has on your life. Thank you for releasing me to the nations to pray. You are truly the apostolic voice of this age.

I want to express my gratitude to Jane Campbell for her belief in this manuscript and her gracious encouragement and wisdom throughout this project. To Ann Weinheimer, thank you for the wonderful help and valuable insights in the editing of this book.

Finally, I want to say thank You, Lord, for reaching down and touching this Southern girl from Rockwall, Texas. Thank You for saving me and allowing me the awesome privilege to partner with You in intercession. To You be all honor, glory and praise! I love You, Lord.

Introduction

THE YEAR 1991 was the beginning of a new and exciting season in my walk with the Lord. A great job opportunity for my husband, Greg, was the initial reason for our move to Houston, Texas, in that year. We soon learned that the Lord had ordained this move to usher us into the call of intercession, prophecy and spiritual warfare prayer.

Before moving to Houston, a strong hunger and passion to know the Lord intimately became my primary focus. I began to spend long periods of time in worship and prayer. As I drew closer to the Lord, He placed prayer burdens on my heart to pray for family members, neighbors and the lost. As a result, a cry arose in my spirit to the Father to use my life to reach those lost and trapped in darkness.

God is faithful to answer prayer! After our move to Houston we became involved in a church that moved in a high level of intercessory prayer. I soon learned about the gift of intercession, which I had never heard of but quickly realized that I was already operating in. The more I learned about all the facets of intercession, the more strongly I desired to see lives changed.

I will never forget the church service that radically changed my prayer life. As our pastor spoke on prayer, he challenged all in attendance to examine our hearts and thoughts toward Satan. He then asked us if we knew God's feelings regarding Satan and proceeded to quote several Scriptures: "The God of peace will soon crush Satan under your feet" (Romans 16:20); "God will crush the heads of his enemies" (Psalm 68:21); "He will crush the oppressor" (Psalm 72:4).

As these verses were being read, it became obvious to me that God desires to completely destroy Satan. Our pastor then explained that if God hates Satan, we also are to abhor Satan and to desire that his works be destroyed. I had never before been challenged in this manner.

Being born and raised as a Southerner, I soon learned that respect was of the utmost importance in my home. The word *hate* was not allowed in my daily vocabulary. This was highly beneficial because it instilled in me the ability to forgive easily. After I was challenged to examine my thoughts concerning Satan, I swiftly came to the realization that my southern manners influenced my feelings and thoughts toward the enemy. I could not truly say that I hated Satan and desired to see his schemes in the earth destroyed. I knew I did not like the enemy, but I also did not abhor him. This had to change. I prayed and asked God to give me hatred toward Satan and all his schemes. From that instant my prayer life began to transform radically. I submitted myself to the mentoring of the prayer leader in our church and began training in deliverance and high-level strategic warfare prayer.

The past twelve years have been extraordinary! I have joined prayer teams throughout the state of Texas and led prayer initiatives in Houston. I have traveled to thirteen nations on strategic warfare "prayer journeys." On some journeys I was a team participant and others the team leader. It is a privilege to partner with the Lord in intercession and warfare for the nations of the world. It is awesome to watch as the Lord brings breakthrough over individuals, situations, cities and nations.

God is calling forth a warrior Bride to plunder the structures of darkness. I believe it is the hour for intercessors to move forward from an intimate place with the Lord into focused warfare prayer that will destroy the works of the enemy. This book is written for those who desire to join in the army of strategic-level spiritual warfare intercessors the Lord is raising up in this hour. Along with specific guidelines, I have included inspirational stories to illustrate the effectiveness of this warfare. It is my prayer that the tools in this book will help equip intercessors for radical breakthrough and transformation as a result of prayer.

1

Explanation
of Spiritual Warfare

MANY OF YOU reading this book are familiar with the term *spiritual warfare*. Others are in the process of learning about this level of intercession. In order to place us all on the same plane of understanding, I want to begin with a definition.

Spiritual warfare refers to an invisible battle in the spiritual realm involving a power confrontation between the Kingdom of God and the kingdom of darkness. My experience concurs with the teaching of Peter Wagner in his book *What the Bible Says about Spiritual Warfare*, that spiritual warfare occurs on three levels. They are ground-level, occult-level and strategic-level spiritual warfare.[1] Let's investigate these further.

Before moving ahead, though, I want to state the importance and necessity of understanding the principles of warfare prayer prior to engaging in this level of intercession. It is vital to recognize the risks of praying without full knowledge. In upcoming chapters I discuss in great detail the ethics required before advancing into a warfare assignment.

Ground-Level Spiritual Warfare

This is the practice of deliverance ministry, which involves breaking demonic influence in an individual.

It occurs on a personal level. As one who functions as a deliverance minister, I have seen incredible breakthrough occur in individuals' lives through this ministry. I have also found that this level of warfare includes spiritual warfare prayer over individuals and situations.

I have witnessed obvious breakthrough over individuals as I have entered into warfare prayer over life situations. The following is an example of ground-level warfare intercession.

As a young mother of three, I remember being bound to the house with a daily routine of feedings, diaper changes, laundry, cooking, kissing little hurts, baths, cleaning and bedtime stories. Those years were precious and I would not exchange one minute I had with my three beautiful daughters. Even so I had a burning desire to know the Lord intimately and to see the lives of the hurting and lost transformed.

During that season of my life, I used the children's naptime for my times of prayer and intercession. The Lord began to place an intercessory burden on my heart for the lost mothers in our neighborhood. One thing I have learned as an intercessor is that the heartbeat of the Father is lost souls. There was one mother that I began to pray for on a daily basis. God is so incredible! As I began to pray for her, she began inquiring about God and seeking counsel from me concerning issues in her home. Asking me to pray when difficult situations arose in her home became a normal occurrence. God was obviously drawing her to Himself.

One day the doorbell rang. I opened the door and there she stood. She asked if we could talk. I instantly welcomed her into our home. She told me that she and her husband were separated and that he was filing for divorce. I told her that I would begin praying that the Lord would restore their marriage. Her reply was, "I do not think that prayer and God can work through these hurts and wounds." I responded, "No hurt or wound is too big for God." I then prayed with her and asked the Lord to restore that marriage, to bring healing to all hurts and wounds and to carry her family through that difficult time.

Over the next few months I prayed for her and her husband. Not only did I ask the Lord to restore their marriage, but I warred over their marriage and began to break every scheme and curse the enemy had placed on this couple. I prayed against division, unforgiveness and every deception the enemy was perpetuating. In the name of Jesus, I broke the lie that this wound was too deep to be healed by God.

Soon our lives went in different directions. I took a part-time job and she took a full-time job.

Even so I continued to pray. One evening we passed each other driving through the neighborhood. She motioned for me to stop and roll down the car window. She then exclaimed, "Keep praying! It is working!" I gladly agreed and continued to pray. Two months later the children and I were swimming at the neighborhood pool. She and her children arrived at the pool and she approached me excitedly.

"Your prayers have worked!" she exclaimed. "My husband returned home last week and he destroyed the divorce papers! God is good. Thank you for praying."

I was thrilled. Not only did God restore the marriage, but this woman also began to attend church and to seek after the Lord. We moved to Colorado several months after this occurred, but I firmly believe that she and her family are on the right track and that God will be faithful to bring each of them to the saving knowledge of Jesus Christ.

Occult-Level Spiritual Warfare

Occult-level spiritual warfare involves opposition to a more structured level of demonic authority. Warfare prayer at this level focuses on witchcraft, satanism, Freemasonry, New Age beliefs, Eastern religions and many other forms of spiritual practices that glorify Satan and his dark angels. Obviously this involves a higher dimension of warfare prayer. I would like to share a powerful example of spiritual breakthrough that occurred in the city of Houston.

Marilyn Manson, a popular heavy metal rock star, travels around the world with his band singing to and glorifying Satan. All band members are required to make name changes. The first name has to be one of a famous actress and the last name one of a known serial killer. The name *Marilyn Manson*, for instance, was inspired by actress Marilyn Monroe and murderer/cult leader Charles Manson. Mr. Manson is also an ordained minister in the Church of Satan. The late Anton Lavey, who founded and served as high priest of the Church of Satan, was the officiating minister in the ordination.

This band decided to come to Houston and the response of the Church in the city was remarkable. Many churches held 24-hour prayer vigils leading up to the concert. They paid for commercial time on Christian radio stations asking people to pray. Prayer groups across the city gathered together and the potentially disastrous effects of the music became the intercessory cry. It was known, for instance, that several youths who had attended concerts by this band had returned home to commit suicide. It was incredible how a corporate burden for the youth of the city came into focus.

I sought the Lord and asked for my intercessory assignment and marching orders in this situation. He told me to form a team and to pray on-site at the theater that was hosting the band's visit. On the day of the concert we went early in the morning to pray. As we prayed the Lord began to impart to us a burden to pray for the salvation of Marilyn Manson, all of the members of his band and the youth attending the concert.

Then the Lord shifted us into warfare prayer. We began to pray that the sound equipment would not work and that the concert would not succeed or be performed to completion. We proclaimed that this music dedicated to Satan would not be sung over the youth of the city. We proclaimed confusion in the enemy's camp and broke every lie that Satan is to be worshiped. I need to add that when we are involved in warfare prayer we never pray against a person but ask the Lord to touch the hearts of those lost in darkness and to bring them to salvation. "For we wrestle not against flesh and blood, but against principalities, against powers, against the rulers of the darkness of this world, against spiritual wickedness in high places" (Ephesians 6:12, KJV). It was an awesome time of prayer.

The night of the concert was an incredible sight. Many Christians were handing Gospel tracts to the youth. An outdoor Christian concert was held across the street. The Lord assigned several pastors and intercessors to pray inside the theater.

The concert began and during the second song something occurred that is still hard to believe. One of the fans accidentally spilled his beer on the soundboard. The whole sound system was ruined. As the microphones no longer worked, the instruments could not be heard, nor could Mr. Manson. It became impossible for him to continue. He became so upset he threw his microphone to the floor, stormed off the stage and never finished the concert. This is not meant as gratitude that a young person was drinking beer, but the incident was a powerful answer to prayer. Within a short time the mayor and city council convened and established a city ordinance forbidding that type of concert in the city. Yes, Lord!

Strategic-Level Spiritual Warfare

This is focused prayer dealing with high-ranking principalities and powers assigned to geographical territories and
social networks. These demonic forces are usually referred to
as territorial spirits. The primary focus of this book will be
strategic-level spiritual warfare and guidelines for those who
desire to move forward in this dimension of prayer. Let's look
at an example of strategic-level spiritual warfare in Scripture
and then a present-day example.

Paul and Silas in Philippi

According to Greek legend, the Greek god Apollo killed
Python, the terrible earth serpent who lived in the caves of
Parnassus in Delphi. He killed Python in retaliation for its
harassment of his mother while she was looking for a place to
give birth to her twins. Because of his act Apollo is at times
referred to as Pythian, predictor of future events.

During Paul's day the people in the region of Philippi believed that Apollo or Pythian was the influencer of events.
The term *python* was used to refer to those through whom
the python spirit spoke. We read in the book of Acts that Paul
entered into spiritual warfare by casting out this python or
fortune-telling spirit from a slave girl (see Acts 16:18). This
caused great turmoil in the city of Philippi. It is my belief
that the response and activities that occurred as a result of
Paul's prayer indicate that the spirit operating through this
young woman was indeed a territorial spirit. Let me explain
what I mean.

Acts 16:19 says that when the owners of the slave girl
realized what had occurred they became greatly disturbed. It
ruined their opportunity to make money from those seeking
information about the future. They seized Paul and Silas and
brought them before the authorities in the marketplace. In
verse 20 the slave owners stated, "These men are Jews, and

are *throwing our city* into an uproar" (emphasis added). I find this accusation highly interesting. Paul addressed a demonic spirit operating through a young girl. Next he was accused of throwing a whole city into an uproar. I have prayed deliverance prayers over many individuals, but never has it resulted in a city uproar.

Then we read in verse 22: "The crowd joined in the attack against Paul and Silas." Not only was the whole city in an uproar, but now a crowd joined in the attack against Paul and Silas. Why would casting out a demon from one girl cause a city uproar and a crowd, who knew nothing of the deliverance, to turn against Paul and Silas? The python spirit operating through this slave girl or spiritist was a territorial spirit that gripped the city of Philippi.

The magistrates ordered that Paul and Silas be flogged and thrown into prison. Locked in an inner cell with their feet fastened in stocks, Paul and Silas began to pray and worship God. Let's investigate what occurred next. "*Suddenly* there was such a *violent earthquake* that the foundations of the prison were shaken. At once *all the prison doors flew open, and everybody's chains came loose*" (Acts 16:26, emphasis added). Wow! As a result of casting out this demonic spirit in a slave girl, a violent earthquake occurred over the region. Not only were Paul's and Silas's chains released, but *everybody's chains* came loose.

When effective spiritual warfare prayer has occurred, signs of what has transpired in the spiritual realm will also manifest in the physical realm—thus, the earthquake. God was shaking the foundational worship of Apollo in that region. The earthquake resulted in *everybody's* chains releasing.

Another indication of effective spiritual warfare prayer is the release of the people of the region from the darkness that has gripped them. They are then free to understand and experience the truth and love of God. Note the breakthrough that occurred in this spiritual warfare encounter in Philippi:

The jailer called for lights, rushed in and fell trembling before Paul and Silas. He then brought them out and asked, "Sirs, what must I do to be saved?" They replied, "Believe in the Lord Jesus, and you will be saved—you and your household." Then they spoke the word of the Lord to him and to all the others in his house. At that hour of the night the jailer took them and washed their wounds; then immediately he and all his family were baptized. The jailer brought them into his house and set a meal before them; he was filled with joy because he had come to believe in God—he and his whole family.

verses 29–34

The most significant demonstration that spiritual breakthrough has occurred over a region is the salvation of those who have been trapped in spiritual darkness by a territorial spirit.

Let's review this spiritual warfare encounter. Paul cast out a python spirit, also called a spirit of divination, from a slave girl. The resulting actions were a city uproar, an angry crowd, the imprisonment of Paul and Silas, a violent earthquake that released everybody's chains and the salvation of the jailer and his family. It is obvious that the spirit in this young woman was indeed a territorial spirit that held this region in darkness.

"Gentlemen's Clubs" in Houston

Isn't it exciting to read about spiritual breakthroughs over a region? Now let's bring it to present-day issues. The following is an example of a breakthrough the Lord worked in the city of Houston.

I was serving as prayer coordinator of Houston House of Prayer, a church we attended while living in Houston. The church was experiencing wonderful times of corporate prayer and intercession. The Lord began to speak to the pastors and me about a new prayer assignment for the church. He was directing us to pray over the "Gentlemen's Clubs" in the city.

There was a particularly dense population of these clubs in the Richmond area of Houston. The Lord then revealed a prayer strategy. We were to pray on-site at these establishments and break the assignment over this territory that the enemy had established through perversion and whoredom.

Wednesday evening was the scheduled time for corporate prayer and intercession. For two months this prayer time took a particular direction. I divided the adults into groups of four to five with a designated prayer leader. Each individual group was assigned a Gentlemen's Club as their prayer focus for that evening and then drove to those particular establishments. I gave specific instruction that we should pray in the parking lots and not go into the clubs. Praying from inside the car was preferable because this was not the safest area of Houston.

One Wednesday I was leading a team of women at our assigned location. As we prayed, our faith level rose and we began to ask God to cause conviction to fall on the men who were going into that particular club. We prayed and declared that the men would not be able to stay in the club, that they would have a strong desire to leave. I learned never to underestimate the power of prayer! As we prayed, a man drove into the parking lot, got out of his car and entered the club building. We were disappointed but not for long. Within ten seconds this same individual abruptly exited the club, ran to his car and quickly drove away. We all wondered if our prayers had affected the scene we had just witnessed.

As the next man began to walk toward the club, our level of faith was definitely high! We prayed that the Lord would cause conviction to fall on him, that his heart would turn toward the Father and his family, and that he would turn and not enter the club. As soon as we finished praying, he approached the entrance. He reached for the door and began to open it, but then he froze. He stood perfectly still for thirty seconds as if in a struggle. Suddenly he turned, ran to his car and drove away so quickly that he left tire marks in the parking lot! "Go, God!" we shouted.

Over this two-month period, we saw exciting, undeniable answers to prayer. Gentlemen's Clubs became the big story on the evening news. Connections and corrupt practices were exposed between the Gentlemen's Clubs and city officials. This forced the closure of several establishments. New laws were put into action. It became illegal for a man to touch or get within three feet of a dancer. To physically place money in a dancer's costume was forbidden and could result in tough legal consequences. The clubs were zoned and not allowed to be built near neighborhoods, schools or churches. This caused business to decrease and the closure of more clubs.

The most exciting news, though, was the breakthrough for evangelists in the city of Houston. Before we prayed on-site for these establishments, few of the women dancers had been reached with the Gospel and brought to salvation. After this season of focused prayer, they began to respond to the Lord and many accepted the gift of salvation. This was the most powerful answer to our prayers.

While some of the Gentlemen's Clubs are still in operation in this area of the city, the demonic structure over this region was weakened as a result of warfare prayer. We were obedient to our assignment, and when it is the Lord's timing He will raise up another group of warriors to break further the darkness in this territory.

Isn't God faithful! Luke 10:19 states, "I have given you authority to trample on snakes and scorpions and to overcome all the power of the enemy; nothing will harm you." It is an awesome thing to see the schemes of the enemy dismantled and God glorified. You, too, can pray and see territories experience transformation. As we move forward, I will be sharing warfare prayer tactics that will help accomplish the goal of spiritual transformation and breakthrough.

Exploring the Essentials

1. Discuss a time when you were involved in ground-level spiritual warfare. What was the result of your prayers?
2. Do you know an individual trapped in occult beliefs and practices? What was the open door for this lie of darkness to grip this person? Pray and ask God to expose the fabrication of deception that has trapped this individual and intercede for complete freedom.
3. Reflect on the city in which you live. Describe an area or location that is gripped by occult issues. What scheme or lie do you think the enemy used to trap this area in darkness? Begin to pray and ask God to loose this area and those trapped in darkness.
4. You can be sure that territorial spirits have gripped your city. What do you think these principalities are?
5. As we move forward into the book, ask the Lord to speak to you regarding issues about your family, your neighborhood, city and state. Ask the Lord to reveal the prayer assignments that He wants to release to individuals and to the group.

2

The Earth Is the Lord's

The earth is the LORD's, and everything in it, the world, and all who live in it; for he founded it upon the seas and established it upon the waters.

Psalm 24:1–2

In the beginning you laid the foundations of the earth, and the heavens are the work of your hands.

Psalm 102:25

When the Most High gave the nations their inheritance, when he divided all mankind, he set up boundaries for the peoples according to the number of the sons of Israel.

Deuteronomy 32:8

When the righteous prosper, the city rejoices; when the wicked perish, there are shouts of joy. Through the blessing of the upright a city is exalted, but by the mouth of the wicked it is destroyed.

Proverbs 11:10–11

GOD CREATED THE earth with exact purposes in mind. Scripture explains: "The heavens declare the glory of God; the skies proclaim the work of his hands" (Psalm 19:1). The earth and the heavens are a manifestation of God's glory, power and majesty. As the vast expanse and beauty of creation are observed, we cannot help but stand in awe of the Lord our Creator. The earth and heavens were also created in order that God might receive the glory and honor that are due His name. "Let the sea resound, and everything in it, the world, and all who live in it. Let the rivers clap their hands, let the mountains sing together for joy" (Psalm 98:7–8). All things conceived through the Word of God at creation, including nature, worship and exalt the Lord.

God is relational. He is not only our Creator but also our Father. He created the earth so that His purposes for humankind can be fulfilled. God fashioned Adam and Eve in His own image because He desired to have a personal and loving relationship with humankind for all eternity. In the book of Revelation, John describes the promise for all believers at the end of history: "He will live with them. They will be his people, and God himself will be with them and be their God" (Revelation 21:3).

God established the earth; moreover, He set the nations in place. He established an inheritance and boundary for all mankind. He is, therefore, concerned about the cities in which we live.

The Bible tells us that all of this is true, but throughout the earth it appears that Satan has complete authority and dominion over people and the land. If God is so concerned with the land, then why are so many people and lands gripped in darkness?

How Satan Takes What Is Not His

It is true that God established the earth and set the nations in place, but from the beginning of time Satan has set himself against the Lord and His plans. And far too often we have played into the hands of the enemy. Satan has no direct authority over the earth or people unless we give it to him. In his book *The Last of the Giants*, George Otis Jr. states:

> Unless individuals give themselves over to the rulership of Satan willingly, they will remain under the tender influence of the Holy Spirit. Satan's objective, then, is to gain control over the lives of human beings by dominating the systems—political, economic and religious—they have created."[1]

If Satan has no authority except what is given to him, how does he gain such control? How has mankind lost sight of God's plans for His creation? Here are four key reasons.

Deception

In the Garden of Eden, Satan was able to deceive Eve into eating the forbidden fruit. She, in turn, once tainted by this lie, was able to convince Adam to join her. The fall of the human race occurred through deception. This is one of Satan's primary weapons of leading people away from God's truth. The Bible teaches that the "god of this age has blinded the minds of unbelievers, so that they cannot see the light of the gospel of the glory of Christ, who is the image of God" (2 Corinthians 4:4). Paul is stating that Satan deceives and blinds the minds of the lost so that they might not understand the Gospel and receive salvation. Deception will also be the dominant instrument used by Satan to lead people into rebellion against God at the end of history (see 2 Thessalonians 2:8–12).

Division

Jesus said, "The thief comes only to steal and kill and destroy; I have come that they may have life, and have it to the full" (John 10:10). Satan will divide people and regions from the truth of the Gospel and a relationship with the Father. He will also divide believers from one another.

Accusation

"For the accuser of our brothers . . . accuses them before our God day and night" (Revelation 12:10). The phrase *accuser of the brethren* is often used to describe Satan. He will accuse us by pointing out our faults and bringing us into self-condemnation. Satan will also stir up accusation from one individual to another, resulting in broken relationships. Hector Torres explains how the enemy works to divide relationships:

> Jealousy, envy, and the spirit of accusation are the greatest weapons for division. The enemy uses this spirit of accusation to bring discord, division, and doubt against our leaders and brothers. When this happens we can be sure it is not from God. God is not the author of confusion, but of peace. Satan can use holy vessels to interfere with God's plan.[2]

Unlawful Possession of a Territory

In his desire to hold regions and territories in darkness, Satan often occupies a land illegally. He does this by defiling the land, thus keeping all those within the boundaries of those territories under the influence of his deceptions and lies.

> When the Lord has finished all his work against Mount Zion and Jerusalem, he will say, "I will punish the king of Assyria for the willful pride of his heart and the haughty look in his eyes. For he says: 'By the strength of my hand I have done this, and by my wisdom, because I have understanding. I removed

the boundaries of nations, I plundered their treasures; like a mighty one I subdued their kings.'"

Isaiah 10:12–13

How does land become defiled? It has to do with stewardship. A steward is a person put in charge of the affairs of a household or estate. God has called us, the Church, His Bride, to be stewards of the land. Genesis 1:28 describes God's thoughts on stewardship:

> God blessed them and said to them, "Be fruitful and increase in number; fill the earth and subdue it. Rule over the fish of the sea and the birds of the air and over every living creature that moves on the ground."

In his book *Releasing Heaven on Earth*, Alistair Petrie explains stewardship of the land:

> This is one of the very first directives given to man by God: "The LORD God took the man and put him in the Garden of Eden to work it and take care of it" (Genesis 2:15). The Hebrew word *shamar* used in this verse has many meanings: to hedge around something, to keep, to guard, to watch as a watchman, to protect. That is our stewardship responsibility—nothing less than *to keep the land*.
>
> Stewardship, then, is a divine principle emphasizing our accepting responsibility for possessions entrusted to us by somebody else, more than our giving away our possessions. This is our personal and corporate call to be stewards of the Kingdom of God. Putting it simply, stewardship speaks of management.[3]

God designed creation for man to manage the land and care for His possessions. After sin entered in, man began to struggle with the land. The enemy gained access, and man began to follow sinful desires and practices. This in turn opened the door for the enemy, with the help of man, to gain control over the Lord's resources.

Satan's Schemes of Defilement

The Bible tells us that we are not to remain uninformed of the wiles of Satan, "in order that Satan might not outwit us. For we are not unaware of his schemes" (2 Corinthians 2:11). If he can impede God's purposes for the land and its inhabitants, he can keep mankind bound to darkness and in broken relationship with the Father. One of the key defenses against the attacks of Satan is to understand his continual efforts and strategies to control the territories of the earth.

Having traveled extensively on Spiritual Warfare Prayer Journeys with Alice Smith of the U.S. Prayer Center, I would like to share the insight I have gained from her teaching and our experiences together. I believe the following illustrations are the primary weapons used by Satan in defiling land.

Shedding of Innocent Blood

The Lord spoke these words to the prophet Jeremiah:

"Go out to the Valley of Ben Hinnom. . . . There proclaim the words I tell you, and say, 'Hear the word of the LORD, O kings of Judah and people of Jerusalem. This is what the LORD Almighty, the God of Israel, says: Listen! I am going to bring a disaster on this place that will make the ears of everyone who hears of it tingle. For they have forsaken me and made this a place of foreign gods; they have burned sacrifices in it to gods that neither they nor their fathers nor the kings of Judah ever knew, and they have filled this place with the blood of the innocent. They have built the high places of Baal to burn their sons in the fire as offerings to Baal—something I did not command or mention, nor did it enter my mind.'"

Jeremiah 19:2–5

Shedding of innocent blood pollutes the land, especially when the bloodshed involves the worship of demon gods and goddesses. When the blood of the innocent is spilled on the land for demonic purposes, Satan then claims the bloodstained land as his own. In an area where this manifestation of demon worship is perpetuated, one will find strong spirits of death, fear, Antichrist and many times witchcraft.

Molech was the pagan god worshiped by the Ammonites. The sacrifice of children was a requirement for his followers (see Leviticus 20:1–5) Many believe that this is the demonic principality responsible for abortion. Through the bloodshed of innocent babies, Satan claims territories.

Satan and his cohorts also claim land in which wars, traumas, shootings and murders have occurred.

Sexual Immorality

Leviticus 18:1–23 defines unlawful sexual relations. Verses 24–25 explain the results of sexual immorality:

> "Do not defile yourselves in any of these ways, because this is how the nations that I am going to drive out before you became defiled. Even the land was defiled; so I punished it for its sin, and the land vomited out its inhabitants."

Remember the story of the Gentlemen's Clubs in chapter 1? Consistent, ungodly sexual practices in a region establish a stronghold of perversion and whoredom. In idolatrous worship the adherents are often required to commit adultery, fornication and prostitution.

Ashtaroth was the demon goddess worshiped by the Sidonians (see 1 Kings 11:33). Evil sexual practices and the sacrifice of infants were her preference:

> Ashtaroth was the wife of both El and Baal who was also her son. She delighted in evil sexual practices and in human sacrifices, including infants. At times Asherah is her sister, while at other times they are synonymous. Ashtaroth ex-

ulted to wade in human blood. She is the personification of demonic powers.[4]

When adultery, fornication and prostitution are propagated in an area, the enemy has gained control and the land is cursed. As shown in the following Scriptures, in which God is speaking through the prophets, the result is the reduction of territory for those involved.

ADULTERY

"[Oholah and Oholibah] have committed adultery and blood is on their hands. They committed adultery with their idols; they even sacrificed their children, whom they bore to me, as food for them. They have also done this to me: At that same time they defiled my sanctuary and desecrated my Sabbaths."

Ezekiel 23:37–38

"If a man divorces his wife and she leaves him and marries another man, should he return to her again? Would not the land be completely defiled? But you have lived as a prostitute with many lovers—would you now return to me?" declares the LORD. "Look up to the barren heights and see. Is there any place where you have not been ravished? By the roadside you sat waiting for lovers, sat like a nomad in the desert. You have defiled the land with your prostitution and wickedness. . . . Because Israel's immorality mattered so little to her, she defiled the land and committed adultery with stone and wood."

Jeremiah 3:1–2, 9

FORNICATION AND PROSTITUTION

"You built a mound for yourself and made a lofty shrine in every public square. At the head of every street you built your lofty shrines and degraded your beauty, offering your body with increasing promiscuity to anyone who passed by. You engaged in prostitution with the Egyptians, your lustful neighbors, and provoked me to anger with your increasing promiscuity. So I stretched out my hand against you and reduced your territory."

Ezekiel 16:24–27

Moving God's Earth Boundaries

Satan is devoted to gaining more and more territory. He will use any method possible to spill blood in order to extend his borders and gather more souls for his kingdom of darkness. Remember he is in competition with God to rule the earth and profess it as his own. He will use human vessels to accomplish this goal. Here is an example of the violent and evil ways of the prince of darkness.

This is what the LORD says: "For three sins of Ammon, even for four, I will not turn back my wrath. Because he ripped open the pregnant women of Gilead in order to extend his borders."

Amos 1:13

Broken Covenants

Covenant is defined as a binding and solemn agreement made by two or more individuals.[5] In the Scriptures the Lord made many covenants with His children. These were not only binding contracts to keep the children of Israel in the purposes of the Lord, they were also a means of protection. Any time a covenant is made with God, Satan will attempt to destroy the pact. He does this chiefly by deception. Once deceived, man then opens the door to defilement by embracing the lies and rebelling against the Lord.

The earth dries up and withers, the world languishes and withers. . . . The earth is defiled by its people; they have disobeyed

the laws, violated the statutes and broken the everlasting covenant. Therefore a curse consumes the earth.

Isaiah 24:4–6

Not Asking God for Wisdom

Throughout Scripture we are told to seek the Lord and follow His ways and the result will be blessing, provision, favor,
protection, etc. As noted in the Scripture below, leaders and
believers who fail to pursue God and His wisdom are actually
rebelling against Him. This leads the Lord to lift His hand
of blessing and protection. These people have allowed their
territory to be sullied by Satan.

"I brought you into a fertile land to eat its fruit and rich
produce. But you came and defiled my land and made my
inheritance detestable. The priests did not ask, 'Where is the
LORD?' Those who deal with the law did not know me; the
leaders rebelled against me. The prophets prophesied by Baal,
following worthless idols."

Jeremiah 2:7–8

Killing of Righteous People

Satan greatly enjoys killing righteous people. He is obsessed
with foiling the plans of God and desires to do so by killing
godly men, women and children. All over the world believers
are being martyred for their faith. The driving forces behind
these deaths are the demon gods and goddesses who are exalted in pagan religions. Satan is in a power play with the
Church and the Kingdom of God. He strives to weaken our
forces by killing the righteous. The good news is his defeat is
guaranteed! Satan will not win!

O God, the nations have invaded your inheritance; they
have defiled your holy temple, they have reduced Jerusalem

to rubble. They have given the dead bodies of your servants as food to the birds of the air, the flesh of your saints to the beasts of the earth. They have poured out blood like water all around Jerusalem, and there is no one to bury the dead.

Psalm 79:1–3

Idolatry

I saved this point for last. You may have noticed in many of the Scripture references above that idolatry is mentioned numerous times. Idolatrous worship is the main reason behind the shedding of innocent blood, adultery, moving God's earth boundaries, changing the laws of God, not asking God for wisdom and killing righteous people. The Lord abhors idol worship as expressed in the first and second Commandments.

"You shall have no other gods before me. You shall not make for yourself an idol in the form of anything in heaven above or on the earth beneath or in the waters below. You shall not bow down to them or worship them; for I, the LORD your God, am a jealous God, punishing the children for the sin of the fathers to the third and fourth generation of those who hate me, but showing love to a thousand generations of those who love me and keep my commandments."

Exodus 20:3–6

The first Commandment (the first sentence above) is directed primarily against the worship of spirits (demons) through spiritism, divination and idolatry. The second Commandment forbids the worship of other gods and any image made of them. It also prohibits making an idol in the image of anything in heaven, meaning the Lord God Himself. The worship of God is not to be directed toward an object; it is based on God's Word—His revelation in

43

the Person of Jesus Christ and a personal relationship with Him.

The following is a scriptural example of idolatry and the anger the Lord has against this practice:

> "The children gather wood, the fathers light the fire, and the women knead the dough and make cakes of bread for the Queen of Heaven. They pour out drink offerings to other gods to provoke me to anger. But am I the one they are provoking? declares the LORD. Are they not rather harming themselves, to their own shame? 'Therefore this is what the Sovereign LORD says: My anger and my wrath will be poured out on this place, on man and beast, on the trees of the field and on the fruit of the ground, and it will burn and not be quenched.'"
>
> Jeremiah 7:18–20

In strategic-level warfare, praying against the principalities behind idol worship and the religious spirits over regions is usually the dominant focus. Idol worship is rampant in the world today. Believe me, this is not just something that we read about in history books or the Bible. It is still very prevalent in our nation and the nations of the world.

I want to address now what seems to be the widespread demonic reason for this ongoing idolatry. It is mentioned in the Scripture quoted above from Jeremiah as a particular focus of God's anger. This tool of Satan has taken many forms over the centuries; it is just as responsible for destroying God's purposes for the earth in our day as it was in Jeremiah's time. It is a principality called the Queen of Heaven.

The Queen of Heaven

In his book *Confronting the Queen of Heaven*, Peter Wagner states: "The Queen of Heaven is the demonic principality who is most responsible under Satan for keeping unbelievers

44

in spiritual darkness."[6] I agree with this statement. The more nations that I travel to and the further I delve into research of these nations, the strongest form of idolatrous worship I have found involves the Queen of Heaven. It usually involves worship of the moon goddess—that is, Diana, Artemis, Beltis, Ishtar or Cybele, to name just a few.

It also takes the form of humans who are then worshiped as gods. I wish there were a gentler way to state this, but one of the most prominent examples of Queen of Heaven worship involves worship of Mary, the mother of Jesus. The enemy has succeeded in infiltrating the Roman Catholic Church with this deception by decreeing that a young servant of the Lord named Mary is "Queen over all things" and can serve as "mediatrix," or mediator between us and Jesus. As the Catholic Catechism states further: "In giving birth you kept your virginity; in your Dormition you did not leave the world, O Mother of God, but were joined to the source of Life. You conceived the living God and, by your prayers, will deliver our souls from death."[7] Mary, "free of every personal sin her whole life long," is also considered to be "all holy."[8]

There are at least two schools of thought in regard to Mary. Protestant denominations say, "Don't worship Mary!" They rarely talk about her. Catholics, on the other hand, say, "We don't worship her, we venerate her." There is indeed a fine line between worship and veneration. But praying to a person, and having statues, paintings, relics and other objects all drawing attention to that person, fall more along the lines of worship.

To be sure, it is important to remember the heroes of the faith. The Bible does this. Mary was the woman God chose out of all the women of all time to give birth to the very Son of God. We can and should celebrate her heart and her "let it be done to me according to Your word" response to God. But Abraham was also chosen by God and we do not worship or venerate him. We need to be cautious not to cross the line into worshiping anyone but God, Jesus and the Holy Spirit.

I think the line has been crossed, unfortunately, by many sincere men and women in relation to Mary. Catholics are taught, for example, to bring their petitions before Mary in prayer so she can present them to her Son, who will be less likely to refuse her. As Pope John Paul II stated in his concluding remarks during a pastoral visit to the Czech Republic, "And now let us pray to the merciful Queen of Heaven."[9]

But it is not the intention of the Lord for us to pray to any person or image besides Him. Isaiah 43:11 says, "I, even I, am the LORD, and apart from me there is no savior." Isaiah 42:8 says, "I am the LORD: that is my name: and my glory will I not give to another, neither my praise to graven images" (KJV).

After traveling to Rome and spending a great deal of time researching the history of the Roman Catholic Church, my eyes were opened to the level of deception concerning Mary. Here is a brief review of that history.

It begins with the Council of Ephesus, which was convened in the year A.D. 431 and led by Pope Celestine I. In this meeting, Mary was exalted to the position of "Mother of God." Note that in Rome at this time, Cybele was the most widely worshiped form of the Queen of Heaven.

The following document explains clearly the deception centered on Mary and how this form of worship was so easily embraced in Rome and the Catholic Church. The name *Mary*, here, refers to the demonic entity.

Mary did not have to undergo a struggle against her pagan competitors; her campaign strategies were much more subtle and refined. . . . [Nor did she have to] confront the ancient goddess by causing conflicts of religious ideas, nor stir up social unrest among their worshippers. Mary simply infiltrated the realm of the former local goddess, assumed her properties, kept the worshippers' mind at ease and thus helped Christianity to gain ever more terrain. All major sanctuaries that had once been dedicated to pagan female divinity were transformed into Christian churches dedicated to Mary. The old holy precepts were kept functioning, although under a new divine ruler.[10]

A note concerning Cybele states:

[P]robably the most venerated of all goddesses in late antiquity, [Cybele] was not succeeded by Mary but by St. Peter, whose church [the Vatican], erected on the site of Magna Mater's [Cybele's] former temple, became the spiritual center of Roman Catholics. In her sanctuary, the most precious stone, a meteorite, was transferred to Rome and venerated as Magna Mater. When Christianity appeared, Cybele's status was most prominent in Rome. Mary's appearance in Rome was definitely supported by the Cybele cult because of the goddess' similarity with her; both were virgin mothers. Since the 4th century, the idea of Mary as the queen of heaven forms part of Christian beliefs and numerous paintings depict Mary being crowned by her son in the company of saints and angels.[11]

Basically what transpired is this. In ancient Rome, the center of Cybele worship was located on what are now the grounds of the Vatican. Worship of Mary replaced the worship of Cybele. Gradually Mary's image took on Cybele's personality and became the center of worship in Rome. In this manner goddess worship was condoned by the Catholic Church and has been perpetuated throughout the world under its blessing.

The darkness that has been allowed through this deception is extensive. Pollution of the land through worship of the principality of the Queen of Heaven (posing as Mary) has led to grievous events for many inhabitants. Here are three that left deep marks on the earth.

Crusaders in the Holy Land

Religions that base their beliefs and worship on the Queen of Heaven often have a long history of bloodshed. In the case of the Catholic Church this bloodshed has been directed toward non-Catholics, and especially toward Jewish people. In 1096, Pope Urban II initiated the first crusade to reclaim Jerusalem from the Muslims for the Catholic Church, which was considered the rightful owner. As the Crusaders advanced across Europe to the Holy Land, they killed Jews and "heretics," with the symbol of the Cross engraved onto their shields and armor.

When the first Crusade reached Jerusalem, six thousand Jews were gathered in a synagogue. The Crusaders set the building on fire, killing all of them. Thirty thousand Muslims were gathered in a mosque and massacred. Blood and dismembered body parts of the dead filled the streets of Jerusalem.

The Spanish Inquisition

The Spanish Inquisition was also the work of the Roman Catholic Church. Queen Isabella I and King Ferdinand were fervent Catholics and brought the Inquisition into Spain in the year 1492 in an attempt to instill religious unity. Because they were both devoutly Roman Catholic, they desired to rid Spain of all non-Catholics. The Inquisition, which lasted for four centuries, tortured and killed all who were accused of being heretics—defined as anyone who disagreed with any Roman Catholic doctrine or papal decree. Parents were encouraged to report their children and children were encouraged to report their parents for any suspicious activity that set itself against Catholic dogma. The number of those who died is not specifically known. Some estimate that more than eight hundred thousand individuals were killed as a result of the Inquisition, while others believe that thousands to tens of thousands died at the hands of the inquisitors. The last murder as part of the Inquisition occurred in the year 1826. The accused was Cayetano Ripoll, a schoolmaster of Rizaffa. The following outlines his trial and death at the hands of the Inquisition tribunal known at this point in history as the Junta.

Ripoll abandoned Christianity for deism but embodied the teachings of Christ, sharing his scanty belongings with the needy and reminding those around him to "do not unto others what you would not have done unto you." Although he did not seek to propagate his personal beliefs, he was denounced to the Junta for not taking his scholars to Mass, for not making them kneel to the passing viaticum and for substituting in his school the phrase *Praise be to God* in place of *Ave Maria purissima*. He was arrested in 1824 and his trial lasted for nearly two years.

Ripoll was given no hearing or opportunity for defense. He was sentenced to be hanged and his body either burned or thrust into unconsecrated ground. After hearing the decision of his accusers, Ripoll stated, "I die reconciled to God and man."

Consider how recent this is! At this writing it was just 178 years ago that a person was killed for not professing Roman Catholicism. This was done in the name of Jesus Christ.

Because Isabella I and Ferdinand were operating under the influence of the Queen of Heaven, the Inquisition left a major stronghold of fear and death over Spain. Those whom the Lord is raising up to break the deception of idolatry and Queen of Heaven worship are currently considered to be members of a cult. They live with persecution. We need to pray for the people of Spain and that salvation will begin to spring forth in this land.

The Holocaust

The Queen of Heaven is a major demonic principality responsible for hatred toward Jewish people and non-acceptance of any denominations that do not focus their worship toward her and the many forms in which she appears. I believe that this adversarial demonic force played a decisive role in the Holocaust. I also believe that it was this spirit at work in the Roman Catholic Church that led to her neutral stance during the Holocaust. Representatives of Jewish organizations and Allied powers begged Pope Pious XII to condemn the actions of the Nazis. But he remained silent throughout World War II in spite of his knowledge of the death camps.

Hitler, who was raised Catholic, sought the blessing of the Catholic Church:

> In 1936, Bishop Berning of Osnabruch had talked with the Fuehrer for over an hour. Hitler assured his lordship there was no fundamental difference between National Socialism and the Catholic Church. Had not the church, he argued, looked on the Jews as parasites and shut them in ghettos?
>
> "I am only doing," he boasted, "what the church has done for fifteen hundred years, only more effectively." Being a Catholic himself, he told Berning, he "admired and wanted to promote Christianity."[12]

My point in relaying this information is not to debate Roman Catholic theology, or to suggest that God has not renewed the hearts of many in the Roman Catholic Church. God is merciful and saves all those who truly seek Him and desire salvation through faith in Jesus Christ. There are many Catholic believers who dearly love and faithfully serve the Lord. The catechism of the Roman Catholic Church states that "God's saving plan was accomplished 'once for all' by the redemptive death of his Son Jesus Christ." It points out that the veneration of Mary "neither takes away anything from nor adds anything to the dignity and efficacy of Christ the one Mediator." In my experience, however, these words do not reflect the heart beliefs of most Roman Catholics in many of the nations in which I have done research and prayed. Worship of Mary as the Queen of Heaven, and reliance on her prayers, prevails by far in most parts of the world over the recognition of Jesus as our sole Mediator.

My point, then, is to shine light on historical truth so that the enemy will no longer be able to keep us bound to the deception of Queen of Heaven worship—in any form where it may appear. I share this information for those who are called to and moving in strategic-level spiritual warfare prayer so that we might see how this principality can get a foothold and maintain power and control. These truths are vital to understand so we can pray accurately and effectively and see the nations deeply affected by these events set free.

Let me show you what I mean. The most supernatural moment I have ever experienced in years of practicing strategic-level spiritual warfare involved the worship of Mary. This experience shows the effectiveness of warfare prayer and research combined together to help loose the enemy's hold over a region.

Santa Maria Maggiore

Having researched this information about the power of the Queen of Heaven to deceive and destroy, Alice Smith and I led a team of 21 intercessors on a warfare prayer journey to Rome. We felt that the bloodshed of the Jewish race was strongly on the Lord's heart as we prayed there. Numerous times we prayed at different locations that lost souls would come to salvation as a result of the blood of these martyrs.

After spending nine days in Rome and praying in scores of churches, I began to understand better the place of Mary worship in the Roman Catholic Church. In all the churches we visited, not one focused on the worship of Jesus Christ. All of them focused on Mary. As a matter of fact, most of the churches depicted Mary on the throne and Jesus and God the Father on either side of her crowning her. She was sitting on the throne of God! Our hearts were grieved for the people trapped in this deception. We also came to a place spiritually where we experienced a righteous indignation toward this false form of worship. In my opinion, as I stated previously, this worship is still the worship of Cybele. I firmly believe that Cybele is the goddess responsible for the deaths of Jews, Protestants and anyone not professing Catholicism as his religion.

On our last day in Rome, our team prayed in the Santa Maria Maggiore, which is Rome's major church dedicated to Mary and is known as the center of the "cult of the virgin."[13] The church was built on the same location of the temple of Juno, pagan goddess and protector of women in childbirth. That pagan temple was built in 375 B.C. and became one of the more important centers in Rome, serving as a place of worship for eight hundred years. Juno is a part of the Queen of Heaven structure.

In A.D. 350, Pope Liberius founded the first church to be located on this site; it was financed by a Roman noble and his wife. This couple was childless and decided to leave their fortune to the Blessed Virgin. She appeared to them in a dream and instructed them to build a church in her honor. According to legend, as a sign that the church was to be erected, the Virgin caused a miraculous snowfall to occur in summer (August 5) on the location that the church was to be built. Pope Liberius witnessed this "miracle."

In A.D. 432, Pope Sixtus rebuilt the church one year after the council of Ephesus convened. This was done in honor of the Virgin's receiving the title of "Theotonos" or "god-bearer." For the past fifteen hundred years this church dedicated to Mary has held three services a day. Not one day has been missed in the service schedule during this time!

As we prayed in the church, a service began. As the people sang, however, we perceived no life or hope. It sounded like a funeral dirge. As we continued to pray around the center altar, a group came up behind us and appeared to be singing in adoration of Mary. One of our team members, Charles Doolittle, commented that it was time to worship the one worthy to be praised, Jesus. Alice instructed me to begin singing *What a Mighty God We Serve*. Our team was scattered throughout the church in groups of four. As I began to sing, the rest of the team responded and praise to Jesus began to fill the church. Please understand that when I am leading a team, I believe it is important to remain discreet and not seek attention. This was a rare occasion for Alice and me, but we knew it was from God. We sang through the chorus a few times and upon finishing, Charles threw his arms in the air and declared that Jesus is the true Son of God and that He is the one to be worshiped. It was a powerful declaration.

After singing we walked through the church on our own "tour" before leaving. I was standing in front of the altar dedicated to the Virgin when I sensed that someone had walked behind me and was standing close to me as if to gain my attention. The Lord instructed me to turn and say hello to the individual. I argued for a moment with the Lord because I was without an interpreter and feared that the individual would not speak English. The Lord scolded me and instructed me to turn and say hello. I quickly obeyed.

I turned to find a sweet older woman who smiled warmly and greeted me excitedly in return. She spoke with a thick accent that I could not place. I gladly exclaimed, "You speak English!" She acknowledged that she did and then proceeded to ask me a question that was the most awesome question I have ever been asked as an intercessor.

She began, "Please, who was the God you were just worshiping? It is not the God that I have been raised to worship and I want to know the God that you and your friends were worshiping. It was so wonderful and free. Who is He?"

I could hardly fight back the tears. I responded, "Jesus Christ, the Son of God."

She said, "I thought that it would be Him. Can you please show me and my daughter how to know Him?" I responded yes with great joy and after she had retrieved her daughter I learned a little more about them.

The mother's name was Maria and her daughter's name was Natasha. They were from Moscow and were Russian Orthodox Jews! So right there in front of the oldest altar in Rome that represented Cybele, the goddess responsible for the deaths of millions of Jews, on the site of a pagan temple, two Jewish women got saved!

Their salvation was strategic-level spiritual warfare in action. It was spiritual birth into the Kingdom of God for which Jesus receives the glory, not a demon goddess named Juno. How awesome it is to serve a God who brought a team of intercessors from Texas and two Russian Orthodox Jewish women together in a church in Rome! I truly believe that the enemy received a major blow in his ranks of principalities and his hold over Rome that day. I thank the Lord for the privilege of partnering with Him in intercession for the nations of the earth. Only God could orchestrate such a supernatural event.

God Desires a Land of His Own

When God called Abraham He stated His purpose clearly:

The LORD had said to Abram, "Leave your country, your people and your father's household and go to the land I will show you. I will make you into a great nation and I will bless you; I will make your name great, and you will be a blessing. I will bless those who bless you, and whoever curses you I will curse; and all peoples on earth will be blessed through you."

Genesis 12:1–3

Abraham was called to be a great nation and it is through him that the nations and the people of the earth are blessed. We are descendants of Abraham through salvation in Jesus Christ.

God's first direction to Abraham was to go to a land set aside for him and the purposes of the Lord. God wanted Abraham in the territory He had established for him. We can learn from the father of nations. God desires His Church to possess the land we occupy and to partner with Him to reclaim what the enemy has stolen throughout the earth. I appreciate the following statements of Watchman Nee from his book *Changed into His Likeness*:

All of God's work for His people is connected with a land. If they were faithful, they possessed it; if not, they lost it. From that land all enemies would be cast out, and they were to occupy it for God. "The land" is the central thought of the Old Testament. God wants a land for His own. . . .

Thus the land is not an end in itself; it stands for the whole earth. God is thinking ultimately in large terms. "Blessed are the meek," says Jesus, "for they shall inherit the earth." This earth of ours, which will come back to God in fullness at the end of this age, is being won back now by the meek. Just as in the Old Testament the land of Israel was a sort of token of God's claim upon the whole earth, so the different portions where His children stand for Him now are a token of His sovereign right to the whole earth today. God wants us not only to preach the Gospel and to edify and build up His Church, He wants us especially to stand on this earth for Him.[14]

God desires for His Church to stand in the earth and walk in the authority bestowed upon us as His children. Note these verses:

LORD, you have assigned me my portion and my cup; you have made my lot secure. The boundary lines have fallen for me in pleasant places; surely I have a delightful inheritance.

Psalm 16:5-6

From one man he made every nation of men, that they should inhabit the whole earth; and he determined the times set for them and the exact places where they should live.

Acts 17:26

God has established boundaries for us. And one of the many ways of regaining our territories that are lost is strategic-level spiritual warfare prayer. You and I are not living in our cities by accident. The Lord has placed each of us in a territory; He has assigned each of us a portion. His plan for His earth remains constant: He desires change to come forth in the territory that we inhabit and lost souls to come to salvation.

The Lord is calling some of us to pray. It is time for those of us called to strategic-level spiritual warfare prayer to know where our boundary lines fall and to respond to the call of transforming prayer.

Exploring the Essentials

1. According to George Otis Jr., what occurs when individuals give themselves to the rulership of Satan?
2. Name a situation in which you discern Satan has gained control.
3. Discuss areas of your neighborhood or city where good stewardship of the land has occurred and poor stewardship has occurred. What do you think has caused this?
4. Discuss a time when you have effectively withstood an attack of Satan.
5. Has idol worship or the exaltation of the Queen of Heaven been established in an area of your life? If so, pray and ask the Lord to forgive you for this false worship. Break ties with idol worship and the Queen of Heaven, and denounce the power in Jesus' name that it has had in your life.
6. Has idol worship or the exaltation of the Queen of Heaven been established in an area of your city? If so, pray and ask the Lord to reveal the root scheme of the enemy that caused this to occur. Tell the Lord that you

desire to see Satan's plan for your city brought down and God's plans established.

7. You have been placed in your neighborhood and city. Do you know the Lord's purposes in this? If not, ask God to reveal His plan for you in this season of your life.

3

Revelation of Assignment

A FTER READING THE first two chapters, many of you might be asking, "Am I called to strategic-level spiritual warfare?" Others might be asking, "How do I know the territory that I have been assigned to?" When we seek the Lord, He is faithful to reveal His agenda and assignments to each of us.

Regarding the second question, we will study in this chapter ways that God might reveal your assigned territory. Regarding the first question, let me state before we go further that not everyone is called to this level of warfare and those who are called are not usually called into every battle.

Deuteronomy 20:5–8 outlines the fact that not everyone should advance into war:

> The officers shall say to the army: "Has anyone built a new house and not dedicated it? Let him go home, or he may die in battle and someone else may dedicate it. Has anyone planted a vineyard and not begun to enjoy it? Let him go

home, or he may die in battle and someone else enjoy it. Has anyone become pledged to a woman and not married her? Let him go home, or he may die in battle and someone else marry her." Then the officers shall add, "Is any man afraid or fainthearted? Let him go home so that his brothers will not become disheartened too."

In Judges 7:2–6 we read that Gideon's army consisted of 32,000 warriors. God chose only 300 to go into battle against the Midianites.

It is critically important that you not enter into warfare that you have not been called into. Yet you can still assist in the effort. The Lord may assign you, for instance, to provide intercessory prayer coverage for the team that is engaged in a battle. This is one of many crucial "supports" for successful strategic intercession. As you follow the Lord's leading you can be sure that you are an integral partner in securing victory in battle!

Some Ways God Might Speak to You

Remember, God made each of us unique and speaks to us in many ways. There is no set pattern. Here are several ways in which the Lord may speak to you to reveal a strategic mission that you are to undertake.

Prayer

As always the best starting place is seeking the Lord through prayer and asking for Him to reveal the prayer assignment. As you draw closer to the Lord in intercession, He will disclose the agendas that He desires you to deal with. Begin to inquire of the Lord the mission He has designated for you. He may expose the assignment through speaking it to you, a word from Scripture or a "knowing" in your spirit.

On a previous trip to Spain, for example, I had a strong sense that the Lord was directing me to lead a warfare team back into that nation. A few months later, as I was in intercession, the Lord spoke to me to go to Spain in April 2004. I was obedient to the direction of the Lord and moved forward in planning the trip.

Dreams

As you pursue a relationship with the Lord through intercession, revelation may begin to come in the form of dreams. As our minds and bodies are still, God is able to speak to us. Many times it takes us being totally at rest for the Lord to communicate clearly with us!

Greg and I were living in Houston and were in a major ministry transition season. As we sought the Lord concerning our next ministry assignment, He began to speak to our oldest daughter, Kendall, and me through dreams. I began to dream of Colorado Springs and Global Harvest Ministries. Kendall began to have dreams of mountains covered in snow. She woke up one morning and told Greg and me that the next place our family would live would be a city located in the mountains that would be covered in snow.

Soon following our daughter's announcement, we had a ministry opportunity in a church in another city in Texas. Kendall's response was, "The city does not have mountains and snow. God told me there would be mountains covered in snow." Within a short time we received a call from Peter and Doris Wagner of Global Harvest Ministries located in Colorado Springs asking my husband to come work for them. Colorado Springs is located in the foothills of the Rocky Mountains! We knew we were to accept this new position because God had already spoken.

It is important to know and understand your dream language, for God will speak to you through it. It is also imperative to record your dreams in a journal. When you have recorded a dream ask the Lord for the meaning and what the different situations and symbols stand for. The Holy Spirit will begin to instruct you in your dream language and the understanding of your dream life will grow and mature. It will also become possible to discern a dream that is from the enemy or your own thought patterns. Remember that God is not a God of confusion or fear. If a dream causes confusion or fear, it is most likely not from God.

Visions

This is revelation the Lord brings visually while you are awake. An open vision occurs when the Lord reveals a spiritual reality to your physical eyes. You might see angels, demons or something like a building that is not yet built in the natural world. A closed vision is one that occurs in what I refer to as your mind's eye. You see the object in your mind. The following is an experience I had with a closed vision.

I was co-leader of a team of six going to Egypt. Before the team departed, God revealed to one of the intercessors that we were to take seven small lapel pins each in the shape of a key. Six were for the team members and the seventh was for the Christian leader who would host the team in Egypt. The intercessor explained that the Lord would reveal to each team member where to plant his or her key. Planting the key was a prophetic act demonstrating that spiritual breakthrough was being unlocked in Egypt.

One night while several of us were up into the wee hours of the morning praying, I had a vision in my mind's eye. In the vision I saw an ancient building with three huge pillars at the entrance. I had never seen this building, but I told the other women in the room what the Lord had revealed. I wrote the details of the vision in my notebook, at that point not understanding what to do with this revelation.

The following morning we headed on our way to pray around the city. Our first stop was the oldest pyramid in

Egypt. As we walked through the entrance, one of the team members recognized it instantly as the building in my vision. She brought my attention to the gate of the entrance, which was constructed of three huge pillars! Needless to say I was excited. The team agreed without question that this was the location for me to go into spiritual warfare prayer and plant my key. This was my assigned territory.

Prophetic Revelation

Many times God will speak a message into your spirit giving specific revelation and direction for your prayer assignment.

I led a prayer journey of nine intercessors into Russia and Ukraine. During our first team meeting, we began to worship and pray. As we moved into the presence of the Lord, He began to speak to several of the team members. We wrote the words down. One of the directions that the Lord spoke was, *There is an underground cemetery dedicated to the Queen of Heaven. This is a key location to pray in Ukraine. You are to pray here.*

As we began to research the area, we discovered the Monastery of the Caves in Kiev, Ukraine. It is called this because it houses an underground cemetery that is dedicated to Mary. The bodies of 120 dead saints, priests, doctors and artists are buried in the caves and many people come from all over Kiev to pray to and worship them. As we interceded in Kiev, this proved to be one of the most strategic sites. We had a powerful time of prayer at this monastery. Appendix D gives the report of this Russia/Ukraine prayer journey. All of the details regarding prayer at this monastery are included in the report.

Strong Desire for the Welfare of Your City

Many intercessors feel an unusual depth of love for the city or area in which they live. This passion, which has been imparted by God, is not always directed toward the physical land; it may be directed toward the inhabitants who are lost and trapped in darkness. This desire for the people to be broken out of darkness and the land to be cleansed is a powerful tool for those called to strategic-level spiritual warfare. The reason we engage in this level of warfare, in fact, is to see those who are lost and separated from the love of Jesus Christ released from the lies of Satan and brought to salvation.

Are You Ready for Battle?

Has God given you an assignment? Has He spoken to you to join a battle? Then the question remains, are you ready? This is an important question. Scripture states,

> The weapons we fight with are not the weapons of the world. On the contrary, they have divine power to demolish strong-holds. We demolish arguments and every pretension that sets itself up against the knowledge of God, and we take captive every thought to make it obedient to Christ. *And we will be ready to punish every act of disobedience, once your obedience is complete.*
>
> 2 Corinthians 10:4–6, emphasis added

Strategic-level warfare is not to be entered into lightly. Make no mistake that when you pray at this level you are engaging in war. I highlighted verse 6 because of the important truth it is stating. As intercessors we must walk in obedience and holiness. I have seen many intercessors enter into warfare prayer before they are spiritually, emotionally or physically prepared. The consequences have been severe; sometimes the backlash from the enemy has been devastating. Anyone who is plagued by fear or takes part in sins like adultery, pornography, lying, even unforgiveness is not ready to enter into warfare prayer. A pure heart is required for this level of intercession.

If we go into battle before we have overcome the giants in our own lives, then the enemy will defuse our efforts and bring a strong counterattack. Peter Wagner's statement in his book *What the Bible Says about Spiritual Warfare* explains this point effectively: "Only foolish or inexperienced people move into spiritual warfare without personal holiness."[1]

Not only is it imperative that you are ready for battle, but your family's readiness is also critical. Your family as a unit has to prepare to withstand the warfare involved in the battle. For those who are married the support and prayer coverage of your spouse is critical. Prayer coverage for your children is a necessity. Before I advance into battle, my husband, Greg, and I are in complete agreement that I am to move forward in the assignment. There have been times when I have entered into warfare prayer and he quickly and wisely instructed me to stop. He knew that in my zeal I was engaging in a battle that was not mine. On the other hand, he has encouraged me to move forward at times when I was uneasy. I appreciate and respect the covering that my husband provides for me as I advance into war.

I know numerous powerful prayer warriors who are unmarried at this time in their lives. Many of them actually have more freedom to travel and intercede as the Lord leads because they do not have a lot of the financial and time restrictions that married couples incur. It is essential that these intercessors stand under the spiritual covering of their pastors or ministry leaders and seek their blessing and confirmation before engaging in warfare. I discuss the importance of spiritual covering further in this chapter.

Not only is family unity important, but spiritual mentoring is key as well. When I first began to respond to the call of deliverance, intercession and strategic-level spiritual warfare prayer, I had no training. While attending a ladies' Bible study taught by Alice Smith, I knew that I was called to learn as much about prayer as I could. She challenged us, "If you want to be involved on the frontlines and know you are called, submit yourself to someone who is in leadership or a seasoned intercessor." It felt as if that statement was made for me. After praying about it for two days I approached Alice and submitted myself to her mentoring and leadership. I have never regretted that move. If you are new and inexperienced, ask God to place a mentor in your life. Submit yourself to the Holy Spirit and a leader and allow God to orchestrate your growth.

Confirming Your Assignment

I have found that as the Lord begins to speak a new warfare agenda, He brings confirmation of the mission. It is essential to ask the Lord to confirm the assignment before moving forward. Many times as intercessors we receive revelation from the Lord and then venture into warfare prayer before we have received confirmation or the Lord's war strategies. Confirmation can come through prophetic words, dreams, Scripture or a release and blessing of those in authority over us.

Several months after I had led the prayer journey to Kiev that I mentioned above, another team of intercessors and leaders planned to intercede in that country. They asked to borrow our research and prayer journey report. I gladly let them read it. The Lord had moved powerfully among us, even connecting us with key leaders who could enable us to pray on the locations that He had assigned to the team.

The intercessors and leaders who were preparing for this new prayer journey were not experienced in strategic-level spiritual warfare prayer. In their excitement and fervor, they decided to pray at the same locations that our team had visited. They dedicated one day of prayer to the Monastery of the Caves. Almost immediately afterward, however, the team members became ill and were not able to pray the following day. This type of physical attack on a team is an obvious indicator that its prayer agenda is self-directed, not God-directed.

I had, for instance, taken our team into the caves to pray on the day of the Feast of the Bones. This worship of the dead was the strongest occult activity I have viewed to date. It is the sacred day when Orthodox men, women and children throughout Kiev travel to the monastery to worship and kiss the bones of the dead. They believe that the bones will emit oil supernaturally and heal everyone who witnesses this "miracle." Remember, the Lord had given us a prophetic word directing us to pray in the caves. Not one team member became ill. We carried the authority to withstand the infirmity and death attached to the caves because it was a God-given assignment. The other team did not.

So please be sure that you are called to an assignment before entering into warfare prayer. If this other team had asked my advice about praying in the caves I would have instructed them to seek the Lord for confirmation. Their eagerness to pray was commendable, but the direction and authority have to be given by the Lord.

I was privileged to be a part of the intercessory team of Operation Ice Castle, a spiritual battle that focused on Mt. Everest in the Himalayas. The Nepalese worship this mountain. In fact the Nepali name for Mt. Everest is *Sagarmatha*, meaning "Mother of the Universe." It is a stronghold for Queen of Heaven worship in Nepal and around the world.

Our team, led by Doris Wagner, prayed in a hotel thirteen thousand feet up into the mountains. We provided prayer coverage for a team of intercessors who climbed to twenty thousand feet on Mt. Everest. This team was led by Ana Mendez, Spiritual Warfare Network Coordinator for southern Mexico.

As the invitation to consider joining this strategic prayer journey was extended to the intercessors of the church in Houston in which I was prayer coordinator, I felt that the Lord was calling me to this assignment. I understood the spiritual weight and cost of this type of warfare trip. So I told no one, not even my husband, that I felt the Lord calling me to accept the invitation. I told the Lord that He would have to bring confirmation through my husband and the pastors of the church before I would move forward. I had to know without any doubt that my desire to go on this prayer journey was from God.

Upon arriving home that evening, Greg asked if I was going to respond to the Lord's calling on this trip. The next morning I received two phone calls. One was from another intercessor in the church asking the same question. The second phone call was from a pastor of the church again asking the exact same question. I had my confirmation. Greg and I prayed for 48 hours and then I responded to the invitation and began to prepare for what proved to be an incredible and weighty prayer journey. God is faithful to confirm His callings!

Spiritual Covering from Your Pastor

The more we move into specific assignments, the more we see that spiritual warfare is serious business. Submission to those in spiritual authority over us is a requirement before moving into strategic-level spiritual warfare. As a staff member of Global Harvest Ministries, I ask Peter and Doris Wagner and Chuck Pierce for their blessing before moving into strategic warfare prayer. When I served as prayer coordinator of Houston House of Prayer, Eddie and Alice Smith were the pastors of the church. I always asked for their covering and blessing before engaging in this level of warfare. If those who are my spiritual covering do not feel that I am to move forward, I do not. If they release me then I gladly press on.

Self-proclaimed prophets and intercessors are not walking under the direction of the Holy Spirit. I have been on teams that include prophets or intercessors who have no spiritual covering. The usual line that you hear from those with unhealthy authority issues is, "I am accountable to God and not to any man." This is a dangerous and unscriptural stand!

Usually these are individuals who have deep wounds from the past. They need to forgive those who have wounded them and receive deliverance and healing from the Lord. These individuals do not make good team members because they usually go against the authority of the team leader throughout the prayer assignment. This can make for an unpleasant experience for the rest of the team. Not to mention that this opens the door for the enemy to unleash a counterattack.

If you are struggling with unhealthy authority issues, ask God to help you. He is the God of healing and deliverance. Submit yourself to your pastor or a deliverance team for prayer. God loves you and desires to set you free from the hurts of the past!

Asking God for the Timing

God is a God of timing. Nehemiah can teach us a great truth about moving forward in God's timing:

> By night I went out through the Valley Gate toward the Jackal Well and the Dung Gate, examining the walls of Jerusalem, which had been broken down, and its gates, which had been destroyed by fire. Then I moved on toward the Fountain Gate and the King's Pool, but there was not enough room for my mount to get through; so I went up the valley by night, examining the wall. Finally, I turned back and reentered through the Valley Gate. The officials did not know where I had gone or what I was doing, because as yet I had said nothing to the Jews or the priests or nobles or officials or any others who would be doing the work.
>
> Nehemiah 2:13–16

Nehemiah understood the call of God to restore the walls of Jerusalem. He had accepted this assignment. Even so he did not decide one day to ride into Jerusalem and announce the mission the Lord had given him. He rode secretly at night and observed the destruction. He gained understanding of the condition of the walls and gates before revealing the restoration strategy. When he released the vision of the rebuilding project to those who would be involved, the word was alive and active. The people of Jerusalem accepted the call and all moved together in unity. When the enemy tried to thwart the rebuilding of the wall, Nehemiah and the Jews were able to remain in unity. They were impenetrable.

As warfare intercessors we need to respond in the same manner. God will reveal an assignment, but it could be weeks, months or years before the timing is right to advance. First Chronicles 12:32 states that the "[sons] of Issachar [were men] who understood the times and knew what Israel should do." We, too, can walk in an "Issachar anointing"—understanding and knowing the seasons we are in and how to pray accordingly. As God begins to disclose a prayer assignment, ask Him for the correct timing. Scripture refers to time in *chronos* time and *kairos* time. *Chronos* time is time in general. *Kairos* time is the strategic moment when something should be done. Moving into warfare before the correct timing is another open door for the enemy. This is where we need each other. If you are uncertain ask your spouse, pastor, spiritual covering or personal intercessors for their input.

I know an intercessor who believed that God was calling her to minister in a particular nation. She received words from more than twenty intercessors and leaders who warned that they did not feel the timing was right for her to advance. She decided to ignore the warnings because God had "called her" and booked her travel arrangements. Not long after her arrival the authorities discovered that she was smuggling Bibles into the country illegally. She was arrested, but she was soon released. Upon her return to the States she boarded another plane and returned to that country. She was arrested immediately. I can note thankfully that she was released, but she went through weeks of confusion and grief over this unfortunate experience.

When God reveals an assignment to us, we have a responsibility to obtain His clear direction as to how it should be carried out. We have to move forward in wisdom and obedience. As we proceed, let's investigate the concept of team dynamics and the importance it plays in a successful warfare prayer initiative.

Exploring the Essentials

1. Discuss a time when the Lord revealed an assignment or prayer mission to you. How did the Lord speak to you?
2. Discuss a time when you witnessed premature advancement into a prayer assignment. What were the results?
3. We cannot advance into battle until we have overcome issues of disobedience in our own lives. Are there areas in your life that the Lord desires you to deal with? Pray and ask the Lord to bring you into a season of victory.
4. As we move forward in a prayer assignment, the Lord will confirm the mission. Discuss a time when the Lord gave clear direction of how to proceed on a mission. Ask the Lord to rekindle the faith that this released into your life.
5. Remember the wisdom Nehemiah showed by waiting for God's *kairos* time to release the plan to rebuild the wall. Has there been an occasion where you felt you moved into an assignment *out* of God's *kairos* time? What was the result?
6. Recall a time when you moved forward *in* God's *kairos* time. What was the result?
7. The Lord desires to reveal His assignments and prayer strategies to you. Begin to ask the Lord to reveal your territory. Tell the Lord you receive His agendas and warfare prayer assignments.

4

Team Dynamics

It would be foolish for one trained soldier to go into a battle against an army of a hundred men. He would surely lose the fight. Just as one man would not enter into a physical war singlehandedly, strategic-level spiritual warfare also requires an army of intercessors. This is war and those who move ahead into battle have to be trained, submitted and prepared as a skilled battalion deployed and ready to face the enemy.

Strategic-level spiritual warfare requires many phases of preparation. As discussed in the previous chapter, revelation of the assignment obviously has to occur. Then comes the release and blessing of our families and spiritual covering. Experience has taught me that the next step, the one we will discuss in this chapter, is securing the team. If you are moving forward as a leader or "general" of a warfare prayer initiative, you are the one responsible for enlisting the intercessors who will partner with you in the assignment. It is important to invite to participate only those who are ready to pray at this level. The following are a few suggestions that will help you form an effective company of warriors.

1. *Pray about whom to ask.* Seek the Lord for those who are called to the campaign.
2. *Invite those with whom you have a history.* This is valuable instruction. I was once a member of a team on which an individual was invited to participate at the last minute. This person was not known by any of the team members; there was no past history or relationship. We did not know the spiritual maturity and emotional condition of this person. Big mistake! We soon became aware of deep, unhealed spiritual wounds—not to mention a strong religious spirit that was prideful and critical. We spent more time in warfare regarding that individual than we did with the principalities we had been called to address!
3. *Invite those who are ready for battle.* As stated in the previous chapter, you cannot come against the giants in the land until you have dealt with the giants in your own life.
4. *Form a team made of those with diverse spiritual gifts.* This makes a strong team and enhances the effectiveness of prayer.
5. *Include a rookie who is ready to enter into warfare prayer.* I am a firm believer in discipleship and mentoring. I always attempt to include an intercessor on a prayer initiative whom the Lord is raising up and who desires to be mentored. Many times these draftees make the best team members. They are eager to learn and hungry to witness the Lord move as a result of prayer.
6. *Select team members with legal authority through the bloodline.* Legal what? An individual with legal authority through his or her bloodline is one who is a descendant of a person responsible for the spiritual condition and atmosphere of the assigned territory. While it is not essential to have such an individual on the team, he or

she carries a large amount of authority and may prove to be a powerful weapon when praying over the land and issues of his or her forefathers. Here is an example of what I mean.

I was privileged to be co-leader of several teams that prayed in key cities in the state of Texas. Anyone familiar with the history of this state knows that Stephen F. Austin is deemed "the Father of Texas." He is highly revered in the state of Texas. While he was a man of greatness, he was also involved in Freemasonry and he structured the foundational tenets of Texas around the beliefs of this secret society. (In chapter 5, I discuss the spiritual issues surrounding Freemasonry.)

One of our team members was a direct descendant of Stephen F. Austin. This bloodline connection proved to be a great asset. As we traveled to specific locations to pray, it was as if a red carpet were rolled out for the team because of this individual's relationship to the Father of Texas.

On one occasion we were admitted into the biggest Masonic temple in Texas and the library beneath. This particular library contains the complete history of Freemasonry, spanning the years from its inception in ancient Egypt right up to the role the Masonic Lodge played in the formation of the state of Texas. Only Masons are allowed to enter this temple and library. Yet not only were we admitted, but we were given permission to research the books in the library and make any photocopies we wanted. We were even able to pray, albeit secretly, in the auditorium where the rituals centered on worshiping the pagan Egyptian goddess and god, Isis and Osiris, occur. This would not have been possible if that intercessor had not been a team member.

There is another benefit to having a team member who has legal authority through the bloodline. Not only might you gain physical access through this bloodline authority, as we did in the example above, but you might also achieve greater spiritual victory in a particular area of cursing.

Nehemiah 1:6-7 states,

"Let your ear be attentive and your eyes open to hear the prayer your servant is praying before you day and night for your servants, the people of Israel. *I confess the sins we Israelites, including myself and my father's house, have committed against you.* We have acted very wickedly toward you. We have not obeyed the commands, decrees and laws you gave your servant Moses."

emphasis added

In this passage Nehemiah repents on behalf of the Israelites, himself and his forefathers. He takes responsibility for the corrupt practices of past generations. This action is termed *identificational repentance.* An individual with legal authority through the bloodline carries the legitimate right to repent for the sinful actions of his or her forefathers and break any resulting defilement or curse over the land. This proves to be a potent weapon in strategic warfare prayer.

> 7. *Be careful of controlling personalities.* Individuals who believe that their way is the only right way may attempt to control the team. These Christians are usually alone in their thinking in other aspects of the faith as well. This is not to say that individuals who tend to be controlling cannot be asked to participate on a team; the necessary ingredient of an invitation is submission to the team leader. Use your discernment and also seek counsel from pastors, elders or other leaders about anyone you are considering. Remember that this information is confidential and for your prayer purposes only.
>
> 8. *Select those with a persevering mind-set and attitude.* In cases like international prayer journeys, the team will be together for many days. Warfare can be intense. There will be instances when the enemy will attempt to wage a counterattack against individual members and the

team as a whole. It is important that the intercessors
have the maturity to handle personality differences
and uncomfortable surroundings or situations without grumbling.

9. *Secure the team before moving forward.* When you invite intercessors to join the team, set a deadline for a
definitive reply. I have had intercessors waiver when
no deadline for a reply was set. This puts undue stress
and uncertainty on the team and team leader as travel
preparations are being made. It is helpful to have the
team membership secure as you move forward.

10. *Get written recommendations from pastors or leaders.* To
ensure that all team members are moving forward under
the blessing of their spiritual covering, ask them to get
a written recommendation from a spiritual leader or
pastor.

11. *Initiate prayer times.* Now that the team is in place, begin
to have prayer times together. If a team member is not
local, gather the rest of the intercessors and include the
individual by use of a speakerphone. Another idea is to
make tape or video records of the meetings and send
copies to the out-of-town team member.

12. *Line up intercessors for the team members.* At this time
I ask each team member to line up a minimum of five
intercessors who agree to cover the team while researching and preparing, while on the prayer journey and
a month following the trip. This is key! These prayer
warriors will provide the team with the prayer coverage
required for this type of initiative.

13. *Strive for unity.* "How good and pleasant it is when
brothers live together in unity!" (Psalm 133:1). The
enemy understands that if the intercessory team is not
walking in unity, its warfare prayer will not be effective. Satan and his cohorts, therefore, will do everything
possible to cause disorder. Behaviors like competition,
jealousy, rebellion against authority, contention, divi-

sion and accusation will begin to surface among team members. Counterattack is a high probability when intercessors engage in strategic-level spiritual warfare.

Unity can be achieved and maintained, however. At the first team meeting, the team leader should explain the ploys of the enemy and the importance of harmony among team members. Once this has been discussed, each member should determine that he or she will walk in agreement with the team leader and other team members. When a team is trained and the leader expresses knowledge and wisdom, it is possible to make correct responses to intense situations. A team covenant, which is signed by the members, provides a great level of accountability and seals the commitment of unity. I have included a copy of a team covenant in Appendix B.

14. Increase through worship. This verse explains it beautifully:

> May the God who gives endurance and encouragement give you a spirit of unity among yourselves as you follow Christ Jesus, so that with one heart and mouth you may glorify the God and Father of our Lord Jesus Christ.
>
> Romans 15:5–6

As the team begins to pray and worship the Lord as one, something incredible begins to happen. While joining in worship and corporately entering into the Holy of Holies, hearts, minds and spirits are knit together. As Chuck Pierce and John Dickson write in their book *Worship Warrior*, "Worship causes us to experience the Father's love."[1] I love this statement. It is in the secret place of worship where love for the Father and one another develops. It is this love that allows the team to move in one accord. This creates a formidable army that the enemy will not be able to devastate.

Through worship, two complementary actions take place that are vital for successful teamwork: The team is built up in faith and the Lord pours out revelation knowledge. The more the team ascends into the heavenly places through prayer and worship, the more this succession of growing faith and divine revelation flows. Chuck Pierce and John Dickson explain this release of faith and revelation through worship:

> There is a progression of faith that comes, I believe, as we worship. The more we ascend, the greater release of faith comes into our spirit man. You have an issue or a burden or a project that you are praying through. You worship and get a piece of the puzzle. God speaks to you during worship. From His voice you war through the next season, and then you gain new ground. You worship more, and you get more revelation. From this revelation, you war. First Timothy 1:18 reads, "According to the prophecies . . . concerning you, that by them you may wage the good warfare." You gain revelation. When you war, you gain more revelation. When you war, eventually you see the project or building completed. I call this the Nehemiah type of faith."[2]

As the team worships, God will reveal strategies for the upcoming battle. This is a natural complement to the next stage of our study: Each revelation will confirm the facts unveiled through research. Now that you understand the principles for gathering and preparing team members, let's see why conducting a historical study of your target area is so important.

Exploring the Essentials

1. What does strategic-level spiritual warfare require?
2. Discuss a time when you were involved in a prayer effort with an effective company of warriors. What made it "work"?

3. What issues in your family line might require identificational repentance?
4. Have you been in a situation that required a persevering
mind-set and attitude? How did the Lord bring you
through this time? What was the outcome?
5. What can team leaders do to help achieve unity among
team members?
6. Have you experienced a time when the Lord either revealed a strategy or brought breakthrough in your life
as a result of worship? Ask the Lord to usher you into
the Holy of Holies so that you might experience new
depths and heights of worship.
7. If you are involved in an intercessory prayer group, what
territorial assignment is the Lord calling the group to?

5

Exposing Hidden Truths

I SOMETIMES HEAR INTERCESSORS comment that instead of researching an area prior to a spiritual warfare campaign, they travel to the location, "feel the land" and ask God to bring prophetic revelation of the enemy's schemes. God is certainly able to reveal issues about a territory as we pray over it, and He often does. I do question, however, our ability to discern "on location" the complete extent of Satan's defilement. Time after time, such as with the breakthrough in Santa Maria Maggiore, miracles happen because the prayer teams are already knowledgeable about the strongholds they will face. When research is done correctly, prayer teams are able to hit the ground running.

In her book *Taking Possession of the Land*, Cindy Tosto explains:

> All through the Israelites' journey to the Promised Land, the Lord instructs his leaders to send spies into the lands

they were getting ready to overtake and possess (see Deut. 1:21–23, Numbers13:3, Joshua 2:1, and Joshua 18:8). These spies went into the land to see the layout of the terrain. They went to see what provisions were available. They also went in to observe the armies they would be going up against. It is always a good idea to know the strengths and weaknesses of your enemy. The information obtained by the spies was used in making decisions for the next step in taking possession of the Promised Land.[1]

Gathering the Data

As your team researches historical facts about its assigned territory, many schemes of the enemy will be exposed. Gradually the issues that require warfare prayer will become evident. It is an exciting and amazing process to witness the unfolding of the enemy's secret agendas over territories. God is always faithful to lead prayer teams to the right book, the right article, the right fact. As you uncover hidden truths, you open the doors of darkness and facilitate greater spiritual breakthrough when you engage in warfare prayer.

The following are suggestions of how to move forward in your research. You might want to divide the topics among team members to make this project easier to accomplish. Here are key areas of study.

Foundational history: It is important to go back as far as you can into the history of the region. What is the earliest known information about the region you are studying? Was the foundational history peaceful or aggressive? Was there bloodshed? Broken covenants?

Original people groups: What people groups fought over or settled in the area? What brought them to this particular area? What were their religious beliefs and practices?

Key historical leaders: Who had the greatest influence in making the key decisions? What were the political and religious practices of these leaders? Was a door of evil opened over the area because of these beliefs?

Historical sites: Which sites in the city have had significance on the people and land over the years? What was the motivation for construction of major sites? What key historical events occurred on the sites?

Religious history: Were the spiritual practices pagan or idolatrous? If so, what gods and goddesses were worshiped? Is the worship of these gods and goddesses still practiced today? How has this pagan worship been adapted into present-day pagan worship? Active temples of pagan worship toward false gods might include worship of the Queen of Heaven, Allah, Buddha, Satan, the gods of Hinduism or Taoism.

Secret Societies: Were any secret societies involved in founding the region? What were the hallmarks of those societies? What influence do those societies have today?

Research Examples

Now that we understand key areas of research, I would like to share two examples that exhibit the type of historical facts to look for. Remember during this process to stay sensitive to the guidance of the Lord. Ask Him for discernment, wisdom and revelation.

The first example shows how religious history, which in this case includes a key leader, will give you valuable information. As stated in previous chapters, I led a team of intercessors into Russia and Ukraine in September 2001. In our research we discovered that Vladimir was a powerful influence in the history and formation of Russia. Traditional history books state that he was responsible for the Christianization of all of

83

Russia, by introducing orthodoxy to the people. Our research began to uncover a different story.

We discovered that Rus, the name of the Russian province during the reign of King Vladimir, was in constant turmoil and disputes with Constantinople. The unrest between them was stirred by the desire to gain more territory. In order to establish peace, Vladimir married a Byzantine princess, the daughter of the king of Constantinople. The king would agree to the union only upon Vladimir's baptism into the Greek Orthodox Church. Vladimir agreed. He was baptized and married the princess.

Upon their immediate return to Rus, Vladimir required all inhabitants to be baptized into Orthodoxy. While on the surface this appears to be a positive move, we found that it had nothing to do with spreading the Gospel of Jesus Christ.

Rus was pagan at this time. The citizens worshiped pagan gods and goddesses in the many shrines and temples dedicated to them. Vladimir, in fact, had been responsible for perpetuating the worship of these demon gods and goddesses. When he suddenly introduced orthodoxy, he was met with resistance. The people had no desire to embrace this new, unknown religion. They wanted to continue to worship Volos, Perun and Mokosha.

In response Vladimir began a season of forced baptism beginning in Novgorod, the oldest city in Russia. Armed troops were sent into the city with orders to baptize the citizens into the Greek Orthodox Church. The troops were commanded to rape women, burn down homes and kill anyone who refused baptism.

The Volga is a river that flows through the center of Novgorod. It is approximately a quarter of a mile in width. When people were killed for refusing to be baptized, their bodies were thrown into the Volga. History reports that the river was so full of dead bodies it was possible to walk across it without touching water.

This action opened a huge door for a spirit of death and fear over the city of Novgorod that has been perpetuated throughout the years. Since that time three other leaders, including Hitler, purged the city of citizens who would not bow to their control. Following the end of World War II, only 42 citizens remained. The Nazis had killed everyone else.

Knowing these truths about Vladimir and the deaths that occurred in Novgorod equipped the team to pray effectively. We were able to deal with the spirits of death and fear that gripped this city. We prayed over the Volga River and anointed it with oil to cleanse the river from the defilement of innocent blood. Our prayers were focused and aimed to hit the mark.

The other example I want to give involves research into secret societies. It is not an exaggeration to say that one particular secret society surfaces more than any other in this type of research, so prevalent is its influence. It is Freemasonry. Many cities and regions around the world were founded by Masons and formed on their beliefs. This was done intentionally in order to lay claim on the land. As a result, the idolatrous worship of the pagan god and goddess Isis and Osiris is perpetuated in those regions. These demonic principalities then claim the territories. In regions that are influenced by Freemasonry, spirits of death, pride, Antichrist, religion and witchcraft are usually quite strong.

Freemasonry has its roots in pagan Egypt. In his book *Free from Freemasonry*, Ron Campbell quotes from Moses Redding's *The Illustrated History of Freemasonry*,

> Egypt has always been the birthplace of the mysteries. It was there that the ceremonies of initiation were first established. It was there that the truth was first veiled in allegory, and the dogmas of religion were first imparted under symbolic forms.[2]

Many symbols used in initiation rituals of Freemasonry are centered on the ancient pagan practices involving Osiris and

Isis. As a result, those participating are involved in idolatrous worship. In chapter 4, I spoke of entering the largest Masonic temple in Texas.

In the sanctuary a black curtain hung from ceiling to floor. Behind this curtain was a huge painting of Isis and Osiris and the all-seeing eye. These images were painted in this sanctuary to acknowledge the powers behind Freemasonry. Even if members of this society do not recognize the significance of the mural, demonic power is released as homage is given to the god and goddess during Masonic rituals and initiation ceremonies. In other words, this is worship of Isis and Osiris.

Freemasonry also releases its members to worship the god of their choice. When initiation occurs, a religious book chosen by the initiate is placed on the altar. If a Christian is the initiate, for instance, a Bible is placed on the altar. If a Muslim is the initiate, the Qur'an will be used.

It is tragic that so many are deceived by the good works performed by this organization. The original beliefs and practices of this social order remain veiled. Be advised, therefore. As I mentioned in chapter 1, Freemasonry involves the second, or occult, level of warfare.

Final Research Tips

Your team will find that the library, bookstores, the Internet and maps are great study tools. As you begin to gather information, I recommend that your team meet for the sole purpose of discussing your research. This often generates further ideas for study. And be sure to establish deadlines for certain topics to be completed.

As the team investigates a particular territory, patterns will begin to surface. Then strategies will begin to form as the enemy's plan for that territory is exposed. It is as if the Lord begins to lay out a blueprint for the prayer journey. It is truly an exciting time.

With these basic areas of research accomplished, your team is ready to start putting the pieces of the research puzzle into place by the process known as spiritual mapping. This is the subject of the next chapter.

Exploring the Essentials

1. Who were the original people groups in your city? What were their beliefs? How and whom did they worship?
2. What are the important historical issues in your city?
3. Who were the founding fathers of your city or state and what were their religious beliefs?
4. Are there pagan temples in your city? Where are they located?
5. How many Masonic temples do you suppose are located in your city?
6. Have you been involved in Freemasonry? Have family members or ancestors—notably founding fathers of your city or state—been involved in Freemasonry? If so, repent for the involvement and renounce all ties to the worship of Isis and Osiris. Destroy or throw away all items connected to Freemasonry.

6

Spiritual Mapping

Spiritual warfare and spiritual mapping work together as a team. In fact, spiritual warfare prayer is much less likely to be effective without the indispensable tool of spiritual mapping. George Otis Jr. explains:

> Fortunately, God has not left us to fight blind. Meaningful intelligence on our communities is readily obtainable through spiritual mapping. As we absorb the benefits of this Spirit-led research, it becomes easier to abandon our primitive hit-and-miss approach to spiritual warfare (sometimes called the piñata method). Fresh insight and understanding release us to economic and effective action.[1]

Yes, God can certainly ordain breakthroughs over regions when we pray, but it is informed intercession—having the necessary facts and revelations as the groundwork of our prayers—that allows for the most effective transformation. As Gary Kinnaman states: "Orthodoxy is necessary, but it is not enough. If it is true that our battle is not against flesh and blood, then we need spiritual insight and power of our own to make a fight of it."[2]

Spiritual mapping is defined as the practice of identifying the spiritual conditions at work in a given community, city or nation. We have learned thus far the importance of gathering objective information (historical facts) and being open to spiritual impressions (prophecy, revelation, words of knowledge, dreams and visions). Now, by prayerfully putting all of this information together, intercessors draw a map that identifies the open doors between the spirit world and the material world.[3] As we will see, these open doors help determine our response as we enter warfare.

In other words, spiritual mapping draws vital conclusions from the historical facts and Spirit-led insights that have been gathered; spiritual warfare is the intercessory assignment based on these conclusions.

Before we move further, I want to stress that God is not calling us to spiritual mapping and warfare so that we can flex our spiritual muscles. George Otis Jr. explains the ultimate purpose for this mapping and subsequent warfare: "The need for spiritual mapping is rooted in its purpose. Large-scale conversions are unlikely to occur unless we discern the nature and origin of obstacles to revival and receive God's prescribed strategies for their removal."[4]

Satan has created these obstacles to the Gospel of Jesus Christ so that those who are lost will not come to salvation. The good news is that Satan's schemes will not succeed. Scripture states that "the one who is in you is greater than the one who is in the world" (1 John 4:4). God has given believers power for evangelism through warfare prayer.

The desired result of spiritual warfare is the redeeming of the land and the salvation of those bound in darkness by territorial spirits. We pray in order to set free those who are gripped by false religions, satanism, mystic religions, Freemasonry, Eastern Star, Islam, witchcraft, Wicca, New Age, atheism, etc. This heart's desire is an essential requirement for intercessors who want to engage in strategic-level spiritual warfare prayer!

Hitting the Bull's-Eye

In recent years I have witnessed in others and experienced myself the excitement, zeal and fervency in prayer that comes as a result of mapping. Granted, any anointed prayer meeting where the Lord speaks and moves is a wonderful experience. But it is awesome to know that because of spiritual mapping your prayers are aimed precisely and hitting the bull's eye! I believe that this is the deeper meaning of James 5:16: "The effectual fervent prayer of a righteous man availeth much" (KJV). In order to pray effectively, we must pray accurately.

I have three beautiful daughters, Kendall, Rebecca and Katie. They all know my "calm voice" and my "you are in trouble" voice. If one of them is disobedient or in danger and I need to get her attention quickly, I am going to call out her name with authority. If I call out the wrong name, authority or not, my child is justified in not responding.

The same is true in spiritual warfare prayer. Knowing the name of the gods, goddesses and territorial spirits over the region in which we are warring adds strength, accuracy and authority to our prayers. If the spirit over a region is a spirit of Antichrist but I address it as a spirit of witchcraft, I have missed the mark. This prayer will not carry authority. The territorial spirit knows that I have not prayed accurately and can continue to hold its grip. This is why I am zealous about the process of spiritual mapping. It enables us to expose the ploys of Satan and his cohorts, to pray knowledgeably and to devastate demonic strongholds over a region.

Determining Key Issues

Now that we understand the importance of spiritual mapping, that is, putting together all of the physical research and
spiritual insight into a clear overview of a particular area,
let's move to the next step: determining which issues should
be focused on in warfare prayer. One trap that intercessors
fall into in strategic-level spiritual warfare is symptomatic
praying. In other words, they focus on the evident problems
in a particular area but never deal with the cause of those
problems. Intercessors must know the difference between
prevailing bondage and root bondage.

Prevailing bondage is the systematic recurrence over time of
spiritual symptoms that indicate a much deeper root bondage.
Root bondage is the original sin committed against the land.
*When researching, mapping and praying, the primary focus should
be uncovering the root bondage.* Let me give you an example
of these two different types of bondage.

The Ute Indians are one of the original people groups in
the state of Colorado. One large population of the Ute was
located in what is now Colorado Springs. These people were
known as brave warriors and very difficult to kill. They were
also involved in Indian wars fought in this area. When this
Indian tribe had to move quickly in the face of danger, they
would leave the old, decrepit tribal members behind to die
alone.

In the year 1848 the first treaty was made between the
United States government and the Indians. The treaty involved
land in Colorado belonging to the Utes; it was broken by the
whites. Within ten years another three treaties were made with
the Utes and broken. Before they knew what had occurred,
the Utes had ceded the best of their land to the whites.

We had not lived in Colorado Springs long before we heard
one of the most commonly spoken statements of those living
here: "I feel so isolated. It is hard to develop relationships
here." I also heard a local pastor state that the divorce rate in

Colorado Springs is an astonishing 70 percent. Now that you know the history of the original people of the land and the broken treaties, do you see the open door? The *root bondage* stems back to the practice of the Ute Indians to abandon the elderly to die alone and to the covenants broken by the white man. The feelings of isolation and the high divorce rate are the resulting symptomatic issues or *prevailing bondage*.

Here is a list of root bondages that have powerful effects on a land and its people.

War

Trauma: The enemy will take advantage of an open door of trauma when great wounding or devastation has unfolded and establish a stronghold. A good example of this is recurring fatal car wrecks in the same location. A spirit of death is in operation on this area. Also, if an individual is involved in a tragic accident many times a spirit of fear or death will attach itself to that person.

Bloodshed, especially bloodshed of the innocent or righteous

Land violations: This is defined as evil or demonic abuse or infringement on the land by Satan for the purpose of gaining more territory. This includes the wrong use of land for satanic worship and altars, occult worship and altars, altars made to demon gods and goddesses, bloodshed, greed, racism, bestiality, etc. The enemy will use these means to pilfer the land that is the Lord's in an attempt to claim it as his own. Many times New Age groups, Satan worshipers and Masons (just to name a few) will place time capsules and worship stones in the land, claiming it for their intent.

Covenants made with darkness: This is a contract or vow made with a demonic being. This could be established by a key historical leader, a people group or a group of individuals involved in a false form of worship. This contract serves as an open door of authority to this entity to perpetuate its influence on the land and its inhabitants.

Demon worship

Broken covenants

Deceptive political/governmental leadership

Early pagan spiritual beliefs and practices

Adultery/sexual immorality

Occult practices

Witchcraft

Freemasonry strongholds

Temples of active idolatrous worship, such as Islamic temples and strongholds and Buddhist temples

Apparition sites: In many places throughout the world supernatural appearances (apparitions) of Mary have occurred. These are nothing more than demonic manifestations of the Queen of Heaven. These apparitions do not bring people to Jesus but promote the worship and adoration of Mary.

Queen of Heaven worship and its adaptations: Diana (Roman); Artemis (Greek); Cybele (Anatolian, that is, Turkish, and Roman); Lilith (Jewish); Sophia (Greek and Russian); Lady in Blue (Texan).

Geometry and Warfare?

What could geometry possibly have to with spiritual mapping and strategic-level spiritual warfare? Quite a lot. The word *geometry* stems from the Greek word *geometria*, which means to measure the earth.[5] Older dictionaries explain the fundamental purpose of geometry as the art of measuring the earth or any distances or dimensions on it.[6] These measurements are achieved through points, lines and planes.

A point is an element in geometry having definite position. A line is defined as the path of a moving point. It has length but not breadth, whether straight or curved. A plane is a surface. A plane can only be realized when two or more of its points are connected by lines, thus forming many different geometric shapes.

Spiritual mapping reveals geometric designs of demonic origin and occupation. In particular, awareness of the design known as a "ley line" is an important component of spiritual mapping. Breaking ley lines is an effective weapon while engaging in spiritual warfare prayer.

The individual credited with the theory of ley lines is English photographer Alfred Watkins.

> Earth Mysteries is a living subject. It isn't simply a study of things in the past. Essentially Earth Mysteries is about our relationship with the earth and how we interact with the landscape and the genius loci (spirit of place). Central to the subject is the concept of "leys," which were "rediscovered" in 1921 by the Hereford antiquarian and pioneer photographer Alfred Watkins. Out riding his horse one day, the surrounding landscape suddenly came "alive" like a flood of ancestral memory. [7]

Mr. Watkins discovered that numerous prehistoric sites, such as standing stones, earthen burial mounds and other like locations, fell into straight lines for miles across the countryside. As a result he spent many years investigating such alignments on the ground and on maps.

The Encarta World Dictionary defines ley lines as straight lines linking ancient landmarks and places of worship. They are believed to follow particular routes and are popularly associated with mystical phenomena. [8] These landmarks are usually located in high points in the landscape.

Spiritually these high points are *power points* or places of energy that have been dedicated to cultic practices or idolatrous worship. Alice Smith defines a ley line as two or more power points that interact with each other and hold the area in a certain kind of bondage, depending on the particular mismanagement of the land. The lines act as a feeding trough, giving the enemy access to the area. Thus, all the territory and people within the plane that is formed by these ley lines and power points are held in bondage.[9]

New Age groups understand the power of ley lines and power points. In *The Skeptic's Dictionary*, Robert Todd Carroll explains New Age beliefs centered on ley lines:

> These New Age occultists believe that there are certain sites on the earth which are filled with special "energy." Stonehenge, Mt. Everest, Ayers Rock in Australia, Nazca in Peru, the Great Pyramid at Giza, Sedona (Arizona), Mutiny Bay, among other places, [are] believed to be places of special energy.
>
> . . . Maps have been produced, however, with lines on them which allegedly mark off special energy spots on the earth. For example, the Seattle Arts Commission gave $5,000 to a group of New Age dowsers, the Geo Group, to do a ley line map of Seattle. Photographs of the result which looks like a defaced satellite photo of the Seattle area, can be purchased for $7.00 from the group. It proudly proclaims that the "project made Seattle the first city on Earth to balance and tune its ley-line system." The Arts Commission has been criticized by skeptical citizens for funding a New Age, pagan sect, but the artwork continues to be displayed on a rotating basis in city-owned buildings within Seattle.
>
> Citizens had every right to be skeptical. Here is what the Geo Group has to say about their project:
>
> "The Vision of the Seattle Ley-Line Project is to heal the Earth energies within the Seattle city limits by identifying ley-line power centers in Seattle, neutralizing negative energies and then amplifying the positive potential of the ley-line power centers. We believe the result will be a decrease in disease and anxiety, an increased sense of wholeness and well-being and the achievement of Seattle's potential as a center of power for good on Spaceship Earth."[10]

This successfully gains my attention! The efforts of this New Age group to increase well-being by healing the "Earth energies" in Seattle, however, have been futile. The crime rate, just as one example, has not decreased. All that has occurred is the increase of divination and demonic power in the city of Seattle.

As the Body of Christ, we have the responsibility of breaking the power of these ley lines and claiming the land for the glory of God! Let's no longer allow the enemy to gain further control over our cities, regions and the nations. The "energies" between power points need to be broken and the land gripped in darkness set free. What do we do when ley lines are uncovered in our research? Plan an effective strategy and pray!

When ley lines are discovered the goal is to break the spiritual power of the enemy that controls the territory. Many times I will pray at each power point that has established the ley line, sever the demonic power from the site and shut the open door that allowed Satan control. There have also been times that I have stood between the power points on the ley line and broken the power of darkness. Listen to the direction of the Lord and He will guide you as to how to move forward.

Here is an example of a recent strategy undertaken by intercessors.

Ley Line Strategy

In 1994, the Lord gave Chuck Pierce a strategic word concerning the city of Houston. In this word, the Lord instructed the intercessors in the city of Houston to be the watchmen on the wall for a three-week period. There was to be continuous prayer coverage during this time. I accepted the word of the Lord and began to pray.

One night after I had been praying, the Lord spoke to me in a dream. I heard the words *Second, Fourth and Sixth Streets.* As I woke, the phrase continued to resound in my spirit. I went to the store and purchased a map of the city of Houston. As I looked at the map, the Lord impressed on me that there was a Masonic lodge on each of these streets serving as power points that formed a triangle. As a result, this area within the triangle was gripped by an Antichrist and witchcraft spirit.

I had never been on those streets, but the Lord spoke it so clearly I knew the information was accurate. I also knew instantly what I was to do with this revelation. I was to go and pray and break the power of those lodges in this area of Houston. This was my assignment during this crucial three-week period for the city.

I gathered a team together and in our research phase we discovered a Masonic lodge at each place that the Lord had revealed! They did indeed form a triangle. Needless to say, the Lord had shown us a root bondage for this area of Houston. We broke the powers between the lodges and over that area. We declared that this was a territory for the Lord and that His purposes would be released. My assignment to break those ley lines was only one piece of the puzzle that the Lord was putting together through prayer, but it was a privilege to serve as He directed. At the end of the three weeks we received many confirmations that the prayers of the intercessors were successful and the enemy's plans thwarted.

Assembling the Data

To review, spiritual mapping is the time when any revelations that the Lord has spoken and the research that the team has done all come together. It is at this time that the strategy for the prayer assignment is birthed. As the facts are mapped, the issues that carry the most spiritual weight over a territory will become clear. Root bondages will be exposed and the resulting patterns of darkness will be unveiled. The Lord will continue to give spiritual insight throughout this process.

Begin now to assemble a team notebook of all the key information. Make copies for all the team members. Be sure to include all of the dreams, Scriptures, visions and prophetic words that the Lord has spoken. Before departing on your prayer journey, make sure that all the necessary information is included in the notebook, and take it with you. This will be an important tool as you make final preparations for your prayer assignment.

Exploring the Essentials

1. How do spiritual warfare and spiritual mapping work together?
2. Have you been involved in a successful assignment involving spiritual warfare and spiritual mapping? Share briefly about the situation and the outcome.
3. According to George Otis Jr., the reason for spiritual mapping is to fulfill the Great Commission and lead lost souls to Christ. Reflect on your city or state. What area could benefit from spiritual mapping and spiritual warfare prayer?
4. Identify issues of prevailing bondage in your city.
5. Identify and discuss the root bondage in your city. (There may be more than one.)
6. Has there been a history of apparitions in your city? Where have these occurred?
7. Consider your city. Do you know of locations that might involve ley lines? What are the power points?

7

Preparing for Battle

THE ASSIGNMENT HAS been accepted. The historical facts have been gathered. The spiritual mapping has taken place. The root bondage has been identified. The notebook has been distributed. Now the team enters its final season of preparation. Before engaging in warfare prayer, intercessors must be prepared both practically and spiritually.

Practical Preparations

Generally with local warfare missions, the practical considerations differ from case to case. Meeting times and places may vary, for instance, depending on the area being covered and the depth of involvement you are called to perform. The Lord will be faithful to reveal the direction of how to move forward on these initiatives.

When I served as prayer coordinator of Houston House of Prayer, I used our mid-week prayer time to focus on local prayer assignments. The Lord walked us through many different seasons. As I stated in chapter 1, we spent several months praying on-site at gentlemen's clubs. We spent time in prayer walks in the neighborhoods surrounding the church. The children and youth of the church loved participating in the prayer walks. I also researched key locations in the city with the help of my assistant. During our Tuesday evening prayer time, I assigned teams to pray at strategic locations in the city that we had discovered through research. Listen to the direction of the Holy Spirit. He will guide you on how to advance.

If the team is traveling, it is time to contact a travel agent, make the travel plans and plan the daily agenda. You may also need to arrange for local transportation to the appropriate prayer sites. Include a copy of the travel agenda and daily agenda in your team notebook.

If the team is traveling abroad, ask your travel agent for information on passports and immunizations needed for the trip. You may need to line up interpreters; if possible, work with a Christian interpreter. It is also a good idea to connect with Christian leaders in the nation to which the team is traveling. Begin to pray that the Lord will connect the team with a Christian leader.

As I was beginning to plan the prayer journey to Russia and Kiev, the team and I began to pray and ask the Lord to connect us with a Christian leader. At the time I was manager of the Arsenal Bookstore located in the World Prayer Center. When we learned that the Christian radio station in Colorado Springs was hosting an Expo for Christian businesses and organizations, I registered our store to participate. Two of the team members for this trip also worked with me in the store. All three of us attended the Expo.

One of the young men on the team began to walk through the auditorium observing the different booths. Almost directly bchind the Arsenal's booth was a booth under the name of "St. James Institute." This young man felt the Lord leading him to talk to the family at the booth. He approached them and learned that St. James is a Christian institute that they founded in Kiev! The vision of this institute is to train the young Christian leaders of this nation.

He also learned that these individuals are members of the church that all three of us attend. The leader of St. James Institute and I talked that evening. It was obvious that this was the Christian leader we had been praying the Lord would connect us with. We developed a friendship and he was able to provide us with a Christian guide and to be there and pray with the team in Kiev. God is a big God! All things are possible through Him.

Not only is it time to make practical preparations, but it is also time to prepare the team spiritually. It is important that you continue to hold prayer and worship meetings as this strengthens the team spiritually for the prayer initiative. In general, I meet with my teams once a month starting six months prior to the prayer journey. Other teams may want to meet more often than that or less. Seek the Lord's guidance for determining your own group strategy. Also invite to these prayer meetings the intercessors who have agreed to cover the team with prayer. This provides an important connection and sense of unity. In addition these prayer warriors need to be kept informed of all team activities so that they have clear direction about how to pray most effectively.

While the team as a whole is joining together for praise and worship, every team member also needs to focus on his or her personal spiritual preparation. Let's turn to that aspect now.

Personal Spiritual Preparation

Before engaging in warfare prayer, intercessors must be prepared personally and spiritually. Spending time in the presence of the Lord each day cultivates an atmosphere in which to hear and receive His instruction. Worshiping the Lord ushers you into His presence. Daily reading of the Word gives guidance and reveals issues the Lord may want you to resolve. "For the word of God is living and active. Sharper than any double-edged sword, it penetrates even to dividing soul and spirit, joints and marrow; it judges the thoughts and attitudes of the heart" (Hebrews 4:12).

During this time, the Lord may take you through the experience of spiritual cleansing. As you spend time in the Lord's presence and in the Word, ask Him to unveil issues you need to overcome before embarking on the prayer assignment. If He exposes a sin in your life, then repent and deal with it. If there are unresolved issues or unforgiveness toward another individual, then repent and go to the person and reconcile.

Seek Pure Motives

I cannot stress enough the importance of pure motives on a warfare assignment. The enemy will try to bring division among the team members. If each individual strives for a pure heart and pure motives before the Lord, the enemy's schemes will be halted. The following is a good checklist for examining one's motives.

HAVING A SERVANT'S HEART

Move forward with a servant's heart. Having an attitude of serving the other team members and the people of the land is a powerful weapon.

HUMBLING YOURSELF

We have all heard that pride comes before a fall. Webster's dictionary defines *humble* as an unassuming character, one in which there is an absence of pride and assertiveness. *Humility* also means an absence of pride or self-assertion. Keep your focus on the Lord and on giving Him the glory for all that is accomplished through prayer. This is key. A great book to read on this subject is *Humility* by C. Peter Wagner.

I would like to add that *pride* and *confidence* are not synonymous. Do not mistake confidence for pride. Confidence and faith in the Lord are necessary ingredients of a prayer assignment.

PREFERRING OTHERS

Keep Philippians 2:3–4 in mind: "Do nothing out of selfish ambition or vain conceit, but in humility consider others better than yourselves. Each of you should look not only to your own interests, but also to the interests of others." Prefer other team members above yourself. Do not seek self-promotion.

GUARDING AGAINST JEALOUSY AND ENVY

When it comes to an important safeguard for team members on prayer assignments, I appreciate the following verses from James 3:14–18. Jealousy and envy are destructive and evil:

> If you harbor bitter envy and selfish ambition in your hearts, do not boast about it or deny the truth. Such "wisdom" does not come down from heaven but is earthly, unspiritual, of the devil. For where you have envy and selfish ambition, there you find disorder and every evil practice. But the wisdom that comes from heaven is first of all pure; then peace-loving, considerate, submissive, full of mercy and good fruit, impartial and sincere. Peacemakers who sow in peace raise a harvest of righteousness.

Live in Holiness

I touched on this topic briefly in chapter 3 and, actually, all of the points above deal with holiness, but I would like to emphasize here certain other aspects of this important topic. Those who have been invited to participate on a prayer assignment should already lead a lifestyle of holiness, but it is essential to deal with open doors of ungodliness in our lives that God reveals during this season of spiritual preparation. Trust me, if we seek Him and ask Him to reveal any open doors leading to sin in our lives, He will be faithful to answer.

First Peter 1:15–16 states, "Just as he who called you is holy, so be holy in all you do; for it is written: 'Be holy, because I am holy.'" Being holy means being consecrated, sacred, set apart. As Christians we must no longer live lives characterized or controlled by sin. We can pray and invite the Holy Spirit to fill us daily and to give us the strength to stand against temptation. As we move forward into warfare prayer, sin issues have to be dealt with. Otherwise we can expect huge casualties of war.

And it is not always the most obvious sins that trap us. Remember: trash in, trash out! What kinds of movies and television programs are you watching? What kinds of music do you listen to? Is the Lord grieved by your choices of entertainment? If we expose ourselves to things that are polluted with sexual overtones and darkness, then we are polluting our minds, wills and emotions. Scripture explains that the eyes are the windows to the soul. "Your eye is a lamp for your body. A pure eye lets sunshine into your soul. But an evil eye shuts out the light and plunges you into darkness" (Matthew 6:22–23, NLT).

If we are going to walk in holiness then we will obey the standards that the Lord has given us in Scripture, and we will obey those in godly authority over our lives. Submissive attitudes and actions are character traits of those walking in obedience. If you do fall into error, remember that instant repentance of sin is another characteristic of holiness.

As we continue to seek a lifestyle of holiness, hatred toward sin will begin to arise within us. Ask God to impart revulsion to sin and the schemes of the enemy in your life!

Conquer Spiritual Laziness

Watch out for a tendency toward laziness. This is the time to set our faces like flint and press into the Lord. Laziness can prevent us from realizing our inheritance and victory in the battle. Hebrews 6:12 explains, "We do not want you to become lazy, but to imitate those who through faith and patience inherit what has been promised."

As warriors we need sharp and clear discernment; laziness can dull our hearing. To quote Barbara Wentroble in *Prophetic Intercession*:

> The Lord has made a way for His people to fine-tune their spirits to the Lord. The writer of the book of Hebrews refers to this when warning against the danger of spiritual laziness:
>
> "Concerning him we have much to say, and it is hard to explain, since you have become dull of hearing. For though by this time you ought to be teachers, you have need again from someone to teach you the elementary principles of the oracles of God, and you have come to need milk and not solid food. For everyone who partakes only of milk is not accustomed to the word of righteousness, for he is a babe. But solid food is for the mature, who because of practice have their senses trained to discern good and evil" (Heb. 5:11–14).[1]

Laziness will cripple any plans of positioning ourselves for a prayer assignment. Keep your senses clear by staying in the presence of the Lord, reading the Word and focusing on worship. This personal discipline is where our ability to hear and receive instruction from the Lord increases.

Overcome Fear

"For God hath not given us the spirit of fear; but of power, and of love, and of a sound mind" (2 Timothy 1:7, KJV).

"For you did not receive a spirit that makes you slave again to fear, but you received the Spirit of sonship. And by him we cry, 'Abba, Father'" (Romans 8:15).

"Fear of man will prove to be a snare, but whoever trusts in the LORD is kept safe" (Proverbs 29:25).

We have all experienced fear, that feeling of anxiety in the face of danger, evil or even pain. Terror is an overwhelming, often paralyzing fear. Fear cripples and disables us in moving forward. It is a snare!

If you have ever watched any of the multitude of movies made about World War II, you have probably seen dramatized the many emotions that soldiers face in battle. I remember seeing a true story about a young man who was so crippled with fear that he hid during skirmishes. He actually lost his vision during battles, only to have it return when the fighting was over. Because he was unable to overcome his fears, he was unable to wage war against his enemy.

It is the same with us as intercessors. If we go into battle overcome with fear, then we will shrink back when it is time to move forward and obtain success.

This does not mean that we will not experience uneasiness in battle. I have been in several situations where the oppression was so strong it felt as if every hair on my body was standing on end. But the team and I were able to move forward because we were prepared spiritually and personally, and we understood the importance of not submitting to the crippling power of fear and the truth that God has not given us a spirit of fear, but of power, love and a sound mind.

Let me note here that there are times when the danger is such that you should not go into battle. The Lord may caution you to pull back. In these instances ask God to bless the people and the land and move on. Never go into battle unless the Lord gives a clear directive. But if you are certain that He is calling you to move forward, then do not let fear be a hindrance to your mission. Fear can paralyze you from being able to make good judgments in the heat of battle, and the results can be devastating.

If you are in battle and begin to face fear, then remember that your response is key. Do not voice the fear. Satan and his cohorts are not omniscient. The enemy may be able to place thoughts in our minds, but he cannot read our minds.

He does not know that he has succeeded in causing us to fear unless we voice it.

Ask the Lord if you are to advance in battle. If you feel you are to move forward, you might begin to quote the truths of the Word of God. A type of prayer, for example, would be: "Lord, I thank You that greater is He that is in me than he that is in the world. Thank You, Lord, that all things are possible to him who believes. Thank You, Lord, that You have called us out of darkness into Your marvelous light. Thank You, Lord, that You have given us a spirit of adoption by which we might cry out 'Abba, Father!' Lord, I thank You that You have ordained this assignment and that You will give us the victory." By declaring Scripture you will find that your faith level rises and will dispel fear.

Worship is also a powerful weapon when facing intensely fearful situations. I mentioned in chapter 2 our warfare assignment to Spain. We prayed in Ronda, a city situated high on a mountain. Its origins are steeped in Mithras worship, which involves the bloody killing of bulls to initiate individuals into the pagan religion. This religion is, by the way, the origin of bullfighting.

The spiritual atmosphere in Ronda is intensely dark. We prayed as the Lord led. When we were ready to leave we had trouble getting out of the parking garage, then could not find our way out of the city. After a long time we finally found the right road. I could see that fear was trying to settle on the team, so I began to worship the Lord. We worshiped and praised the entire 45-minute drive down the steep and windy mountain roads. By the time we reached the bottom of the mountain all of us were laughing and rejoicing in the Lord. Worship ushers us into the presence of the Lord and breaks the back of fear.

If you struggle with fear in general, ask God to reveal the cause and pray for deliverance. God gave me complete freedom from fear in my own life.

When we were children, my sister and I were staying at a childcare facility near our home while our parents went to a Dallas Cowboys football game with friends. She was six years old; I was three. While climbing on the monkey bars, I fell and broke my elbow. Cell phones did not exist at this time, so the caretaker was unable to reach my parents. I continued to cry uncontrollably and she was unable to calm me.

Frustrated, she placed me in a crib in a dark room and refused to allow my distraught sister to be with me. I still remember my sister standing in the doorway of the room wanting to come to me and not being allowed to do so. I was in pain and frightened. Needless to say, when my parents arrived to pick us up they were not happy and we never stayed there again.

As a result of that incident, I became terrified of heights and the dark. From that time until I was delivered from fear as an adult, I was plagued with nightmares. Even after Greg and I were married and had our first child, fear had a grip on me. If he was traveling out of town on business, I could not sleep unless the television, radio and every light in the house were on. When I traveled by plane, I had to take enough Dramamine to put me to sleep. I could not stand ladders or balconies.

As the Lord began to teach me about intercession, deliverance and warfare, I realized I had to deal with these fears. How could I cast out a spirit of fear in another individual if I was walking in fear? How could I go to the places and nations the Lord was revealing to me in prayer if I was afraid of heights and flying? I began to cry out to the Lord for freedom. One time at a women's retreat, one of the speakers asked all of the women with fear issues to stand. He prayed over us corporately and broke the spirit of fear. I felt as if something perched on my shoulders left. I was thrilled!

When I returned home I knew I had been set free. Even so, I quickly learned that I was going to have to stand in my deliverance to keep the victory.

Every night for two months, I dealt with a spirit of fear. I could feel when the spirit would enter our home at night while we slept. Instead of covering my head with the covers or scooting closer to my husband for comfort, I would get out of bed, walk to the family room and address that spirit of fear. Even though I could not see it, I would walk to where I felt its presence the strongest and address it as if I were staring it in the eyes. I told it to leave in the name of Jesus and never come back. It was not welcome in my life or home any longer. I told fear that it would not touch my child or my husband.

During this time I spent many hours in the middle of the night praying. Even when I was worshiping the Lord and moving into intercession, that spirit of fear would try to return. I would rise from the floor and walk to the spot where I could feel the presence of fear and address it face to face.

Greg left town on a business trip. This was the true test! At night, after putting my daughter to bed, I turned off all the lights. The television and radio were off and I proclaimed, "I am not submitting to fear any longer! I will not embrace you, spirit of fear!" Guess what? I was not afraid! Since that time, darkness and dark places do not bother me and I have been able to fly without hesitation. God is faithful to set us free from the snares of the enemy that entangle us!

Positioned as a Soldier

Personal preparation for warfare means embracing the idea of being a soldier for the Kingdom. Matthew 11:12 describes the stance of a warfare intercessor, "From the days of John the Baptist until now, the kingdom of heaven has been forcefully advancing, and forceful men lay hold of it." The original Greek word for *force* is *biastes*. It means to take something in an energetic and aggressive manner. It is forceful, powerful, vigorous. Soldiers in the army of God are tenacious in spirit and press forward vigorously in the authority given to us by God. As warfare intercessors, we carry the burden until breakthrough and victory have occurred. In order to achieve this goal, warfare intercessors must understand the battle plan, know the Father's heart and use great wisdom and discernment.

Ephesians 6:12 states, "For our struggle is not against flesh and blood, but against the rulers, against the authorities, against the powers of this dark world and against the spiritual forces of evil in the heavenly realms." As we engage in spiritual warfare, we realize that our battle is not against an individual or people group; it is against Satan and his cohorts. Even so, we can learn a great deal from men and women who fight in physical wars. Any great leader studies the tactics of the enemy and usually holds a certain respect toward the enemy's war strategies. No battle plan is effective without this comprehension.

Warfare intercessors need to move forward with an understanding that this is war! It is not a time to move forward with a nonchalant or presumptuous attitude. Presumption is sin and an open door. Satan is a formidable enemy and to enter battle without a certain acknowledgment of his evil power is foolhardy. Notice that I am not suggesting that we admire him or his deceptive ways; I am saying that wisdom of his schemes and knowing when and how to address territorial spirits is crucial. Ask God to impart wisdom in this season of preparation.

Soldiers entering into battle understand that death is a possibility. Those who engage in spiritual warfare prayer walk in unconditional obedience to the Lord and do not love their lives unto death. Unto *death*? While I understand this is an extreme statement to make, it is a requirement of a soldier. I do not believe that God sends us into battle to die, but I do believe that as warfare intercessors we have to come to terms with the dangers of battle. There are casualties in war. As we abandon ourselves to Him and lay our lives before Him, we will find within ourselves a desire and passion to follow the

Lord no matter the cost, and we learn to love not our lives even unto death.

Weigh the Cost

Are you willing to follow Me no matter the cost?
I will never forget the night the Lord asked me this question. I had submitted my name for the first time to participate on a warfare prayer journey. The trip was to Nigeria. The church I attended required those interested in participating on the prayer journey to fill out an application and go through an interview process. It was several nights before the interview and I was in intercession until the wee hours of the morning. The Lord began to speak to me about spiritual warfare prayer and the nations. He asked, *Are you willing to travel to the nations of the earth to pray?* I responded, "Yes, Lord." He asked, *Are you willing to follow Me no matter the cost?* I answered, "Lord, I want to say yes. Help me to have the strength to say yes." He then asked, *Do you love not your life unto death?* I wanted so badly to tell Him that I was willing to give my life, but an intense struggle was going on inside of me.

Over the next few days, I began to cry out to the Lord to give me the strength to follow Him. The night before my scheduled interview, I was able to answer God and tell Him that I wanted to follow Him no matter the cost. I asked Him to give me the strength to do this. It was a powerful time of prayer, and I thought that I had resolved this issue in my spirit.

I went for the interview the next day and things were proceeding well. As the last question was asked, I understood why the struggle of the previous few days had occurred. Alice Smith looked right at me and asked, "Are you willing to give your life for the Lord?"

I answered, "I knew you were going to ask that question! I have been before the Lord the past few days and crying out for the strength to say yes. The best that I can answer is I have told the Lord that I desire to follow Him no matter the cost and have asked Him to give me the strength to do so."

I was not chosen as a team member for this trip. As I understood later, the Lord was using this process to prepare me for future warfare assignments. It was a time in my life of deep soul searching and truly laying my life's agendas before the Lord and accepting His plan for my life.

At the time, however, I really felt that this was a resolved issue. Then a few months later our pastor preached a message that pierced my heart. He began to challenge the congregation to deeper commitment and shared incredible stories of men and women who were faithful to the Lord until the end. I knew as he preached this inspiring message that I had not completely settled the issue. Day after day I got on my knees before the Lord and cried out, "Lord, make me faithful to the end." I had weighed the cost and wanted to commit fully so that I could go to the nations and pray. I told no one, not even my husband, about this burden. It was between me and God.

Three weeks into this time with the Lord, I attended a meeting for the intercessors who pray regularly for Eddie and Alice Smith. The Lord had told Alice to bless their intercessors in this meeting. She began to pray and prophesy over each of us. As she looked at me she called my name and pointed her finger toward me. It felt as if the Lord were standing in front of me. She looked right in my eyes and declared, "The Lord says you will be faithful to the end!" That word shot through me. It penetrated every part of my being. I began to tremble. She then said, "The Lord has given you this word, so when you are in intense situations you can grab hold of it and know that you will be faithful no matter the cost."

After that evening the Lord began to release me into strategic-level spiritual warfare prayer. I began to experience deeper levels of intercession in my prayer closet. Invitations were now extended to me to participate on warfare prayer assignments in my city, state and then to the nations. I can honestly say that I have been in intense and dangerous situations since this word was spoken to me. Because the word is alive in my spirit, I do not let fear keep me from moving forward and pressing into the call the Lord has placed on my life.

Take Up the Armor of God

Every soldier goes into battle with his armor in place. Ephesians 6:13–17 explains the armor that Christians use in our battle against evil:

> Therefore put on the full armor of God, so that when the day of evil comes, you may be able to stand your ground, and after you have done everything, to stand. Stand firm then, with the belt of truth buckled around your waist, with the breastplate of righteousness in place, and with your feet fitted with the readiness that comes from the gospel of peace. In addition to all this, take up the shield of faith, with which you can extinguish all the flaming arrows of the evil one. Take the helmet of salvation and the sword of the Spirit, which is the word of God.

We must learn to walk in the armor of God. It protects us and helps us to maneuver through life.

It is possible to get holes in our armor by events that take place in our daily lives. Hurts inflicted by another person or a traumatic situation that causes our faith to stagger are just two examples. When something like this happens, submit yourself to others for prayer and resolve the issue.

I want to add a word of caution about putting on the armor. For some individuals this important protection takes on a superstitious format. In these cases, putting on the armor actually becomes a form of idolatry. They feel that chanting certain expressions or incantations over and over, in this case listing the parts of the armor, gives them power. I have been with intercessors who will not advance into warfare prayer until they have religiously put on the armor of God; they believe that this gives them power for war.

It is right and good to speak forth truths from Scripture in order to impart faith, but when we feel we have to pray these words before advancing into battle and will not press forward unless doing so, we are following a superstitious practice. We are then walking in the same mind-set as those gripped in idolatrous and superstitious forms of worship that we are sent to war against.

Spending time in the Lord's presence and the Word of God is the place we are equipped and clothed in the armor of God. It is a growth process. As we grow in our relationship with the Lord through prayer, as we read the Word and it becomes sharp and active in our lives, as we enter the Holy of Holies in worship, we are purified. The Lord clothes us in His presence and the armor of God becomes a part of our daily spiritual wardrobe. Once we have submitted to this process, I believe exactly as Paul directs, that we put on the armor and stand in it. It is a matter of understanding our authority, choice, lifestyle and faith.

Maintain Faith for Breakthrough

Hebrews 11 is known as the "faith hall of fame." It is humbling to read this chapter of the ancients and see what was accomplished for the Kingdom of God through faith. Hebrews 11:1–2 explains the faith necessary for breakthrough. "Now faith is being sure of what we hope for and certain of what we do not see. This is what the ancients were commended for." Just as faith was required of Abraham, Noah, Moses, Enoch, Gideon and the other great men and women of God to receive the inheritance and promise of God, it is also required of us as prayer warriors.

As you pray for spiritual breakthrough for your mission, be mindful of the fact that negative attitudes can affect the outcome. Lack of confidence in the Lord, doubt in your spiritual authority and nagging prayer concerns can all undermine your faith.

Faith is the necessary ingredient in warfare intercession to bring spiritual breakthrough. As we daily walk with God our faith in Him grows, but I believe that faith is also a choice. Second Peter 1:3 states, "His divine power has given us *everything* we need for life and godliness through our knowledge of him who called us by his own glory and goodness" (emphasis added). In this verse Peter explains that God has given us everything needed for our Christian walks. This tells me that if we choose to believe what Scripture says, then we have the necessary tools to move forward in all we do.

Luke 10:19 explains, "Behold, I give unto you power to tread on serpents and scorpions, and over all the power of the enemy: and nothing shall by any means hurt you" (KJV). The Greek word for *tread* is *pateo*. The Enhanced Strong's Lexicon gives the following definitions:

To trample

Crush with the feet

To advance by setting foot upon, tread upon

To encounter successfully the greatest perils from the machinations and persecutions with which Satan would fain thwart the preaching of the Gospel

Jesus Himself tells us that we have the authority to tread on darkness and to defeat the schemes of the enemy. We have the power to tear down strongholds and to set the captive free.

Even so Luke 10:20 continues with, "However, do not rejoice that the spirits submit to you, but rejoice that your names are written in heaven." This keeps our authority in appropriate perspective and our hearts and minds focused on the precedence of salvation of lost souls. Remember that salvation of the lost is the reason why we war in the heavenlies. We rejoice in this fact.

During this season of physical and spiritual preparation ask the Lord to impart faith to you where faith is lacking. Ask Him to increase your confidence for the prayer assignment and to give you a focused and tenacious spirit and passion for the salvation of lost souls. Choose to walk in the authority given to you by the Lord. Advance with the attitude of a soldier. He has called us to move forward in faith and boldness to break strongholds from the land so that souls trapped in darkness may come to salvation.

Now we are ready to enter the war.

Exploring the Essentials

1. In what areas do intercessors need to be prepared before engaging in warfare prayer? Are you prepared for a warfare assignment?
2. Investigate further: Examine your motives. Are there areas that you need to work on? Pray and ask God to help you gain victory in these areas.
3. What daily practices give you strength to stand against temptation?
4. Are there areas in your life where laziness is an issue? Ask God to forgive you for laziness and procrastination. Ask Him to give you strength to press through these issues.
5. What is the result of an intercessor going into battle while struggling personally with fear?
6. Are there fear issues in your life? Ask the Lord to reveal and deal with them. Praise and thank the Lord for the victory in this area.
7. Has the Lord asked you to follow Him at any cost? What has the Lord asked you to lay down?

8

Advancing into Battle

T HE TIME HAS come to advance! Now the battle begins. In this chapter I am not attempting to put God in a box and insist that you follow this model step by step. Legalism is detrimental to warfare prayer! I am giving suggestions and examples from my experiences with effective on-site warfare prayer.

The most important point to remember is to be obedient to the leading of the Holy Spirit and pray accordingly. He will tell your team what to deal with and what not to deal with in warfare prayer. Many times the locations that you think will be the most intense will not be and the locations you think will not carry a significant spiritual weight will. Some of the locations on the agenda might not even require prayer. I have been on teams numerous times when it became obvious that we were not to pray at a particular location. Your job might be simply to spy out the land. Or perhaps another group of intercessors has already broken the darkness of that place.

Demonic spiritual forces over a territory consist of many levels. It is much like the structure of an onion: There are many layers to peel before you uncover the core. Even though you have identified the root bondage in the spiritual mapping phase of your preparation, you will face many levels of darkness before you arrive at that deep level. Strategize accordingly. Ask the Lord to unfold the strategy of how to pray effectively and see each level of darkness exposed and dealt with all the way to the root issue. Keep in mind you might be the first group of intercessors on the land to engage in warfare prayer. This is great. You will feel, however, that you are just beginning to chisel away at the foundation of darkness the enemy has perpetuated in the region. Do not become discouraged but pray faithfully through your assignment. God will raise up other intercessors to follow who will continue to deal with and war against the established strongholds of the region.

It was obvious, for instance, on our prayer journey to Russia and Ukraine that strategic warfare prayer had not occurred on some of the locations where God directed us to pray. We discerned this at the beginning of the prayer journey and knew that we were the first to pray at this level at many of the sites. But this did not deter us one bit from the Lord's agenda. We prayed and warred as the Lord led, knowing that we were paving the way for the next team of prayer warriors. On the other hand, the opposite can happen. Your team might be the group that will issue the final blow against the powers of darkness and transformation will begin to flow. Each layer removed is an important step gained for the Kingdom of God and crucial for breakthrough.

If you are on an extended prayer journey, remember to remain flexible. Information that was not uncovered in the research will begin to be exposed. More times than not, the Lord will redirect or change the daily agenda. Begin each day with prayer and be sensitive to the Lord's leading.

Here are nineteen suggestions for effective on-site warfare prayer.

1. Use discernment.

When arriving at a warfare prayer location, discern the spiritual and physical conditions of the area. Listen for further revelation from the Lord. If you have a guide, ask him or her to share any historical and spiritual facts about the location. Many times a casual statement can prove to be a vital piece of information for a prayer team.

2. Pray out of obedience.

After using the tools of discernment and observation, pull your team together and begin to pray. Base your prayers on obedience, not feelings. When the team has reached a consensus on the direction to take, follow that direction.

3. Pray with your eyes open.

A trained soldier would not go into battle with his eyes closed and expect to aim his weapon with any accuracy. A soldier is alert and aware of all that is happening around him.

While on a warfare trip to Egypt, I was given an assignment to take pictures in the Valley of the Kings. I needed to purchase more batteries for my camera, so another team member named Steve and I went into a small gift shop adjacent to the tour bus parking lot. This is a good time to state that if you are in a foreign nation, always have a travel partner with you. Never venture out on your own. It can be dangerous.

After purchasing the batteries, Steve and I walked out of the store and toward the bus. I was busy loading the batteries into my camera and not paying attention to my surroundings. Suddenly Steve pushed me hard causing me to stumble forward. Before I could say anything he pushed me again. Finally I turned to Steve for an explanation of his odd behavior and realized that I had almost walked into the midst of a group of men with machine guns. They were soldiers guarding a civilian in the center of the circle. Their guns were aimed and ready to fire. If Steve had not pushed me forcibly out of the way, I would have walked right into the line of fire.

We got on the bus quickly and Alice Smith, the team leader, rightfully fussed at me. Always be alert when in warfare or unfamiliar surroundings.

Another reason why I prefer to pray with open eyes in warfare prayer is an issue of reverence. When praying to God, closing your eyes and bowing your head shows respect and worship. Why would I want to close my eyes and bow my head when addressing Satan and his cohorts! I choose to pray with my eyes open and in an authoritative manner when dealing with the enemy.

Lastly, closing your eyes while praying might cause you to miss a miraculous occurrence.

4. Pray in close proximity to the team members.
Stand closely to each other so you can hear all that is being prayed. You will want to be praying in agreement and this is impossible if you cannot hear what is being said.

5. Read aloud the Scriptures that the Lord has revealed and is revealing. Many times He will reveal Scriptures that carry a prophetic message or declaration that needs to be released while you are praying on-site. The Word of God is sharper than any double-edged sword, and speaking His truth through His Word creates an atmosphere for breakthrough.

6. Pray through all the key information that the Lord revealed in the research. Be sensitive to the leading of the Holy Spirit at each site. Pray through the research that is relevant to each location. As you proceed into the warfare initiative, your understanding of the history and spiritual condition of the land will grow. As you move from one site to the next, more of the research facts and prophetic revelation will be addressed.

7. Repent for the defilement of the land.
Do not forget identificational repentance. This was discussed in chapter 4. If a team member has legal right through

the bloodline to repent on behalf of his or her forefathers, he or she should repent as the Lord leads.

8. Remember that in some locations you will enter into warfare prayer and others you will not.

This requires discernment. Get the agenda of the Lord before praying. When not engaged in warfare prayer ask the Lord to bless the land and its inhabitants and to bring them to salvation. On certain locations you may ask God to battle or to send His angels to battle on behalf of the land and the people. There will be locations where you are not led to do anything. Do not become legalistic and feel you have to do warfare on every location you researched. Pray a simple prayer and move on. Listen to the leading of the Holy Spirit. He will reveal the correct stance to take in prayer.

9. Break the power of defilement and sever all ties the territorial spirit has on this location.

If I were addressing the goddess Isis in warfare prayer, for instance, this is an example of how I would pray. Please remember this is an example. God will direct your praying while on the prayer assignment.

> In the name of Jesus I come against the stronghold and demonic worship of Isis. You have been exposed and found out. I address every witchcraft and Antichrist spirit attached to the worship of Isis and the Queen of Heaven structure. Every spirit of error, lying, death, unbelief and fear associated with the worship of this demon goddess, I now break you off of this land and the people in the name of Jesus. I come against every scheme and agenda you have perpetuated on this land and its inhabitants. You will no longer be worshiped or speak forth your lies and deceit. Your assignment on this land is cancelled and nullified. It is over and finished. I command you now in the name of Jesus to leave! You have been handed your eviction notice!

10. Never pray against a person; pray against the principalities that have gripped the region.

First, a word about principalities. Remember that in strategic-level warfare you will face principalities, also called territorial spirits. You might also deal with demonic strongholds in the region that have gripped individuals as a result of a principality, but strategic warfare deals with a more structured level.

Some teach that intercessors have been needlessly harmed as a result of addressing territorial spirits. This is true. Some individuals have experienced excessive and devastating counterattack from the enemy as a result of warring against principalities. In my experience, however, those who have received extreme backlash stepped out without a release from the Lord, did not have proper covering or moved forward out of God's timing. Wisdom from the Lord is paramount. If God calls you to a warfare campaign, He will give you the wisdom and understanding to carry it through successfully. Never enter into warfare presumptuously.

And never pray against a person. While in Kiev we prayed in a region that was gripped by fear of an Orthodox priest who also practiced witchcraft. The people living in his village and the surrounding villages were spellbound by fear from his lies.

Pastors and evangelists had been trying to reach this region with the Gospel for years. Whenever the villagers attended evangelistic meetings they would respond to the Gospel message and receive salvation. But following the departure of the pastors and evangelists, this priest would visit every home in which a salvation experience had occurred. He would tell the people that they had fallen prey to a false religion and that if they did not denounce the experience and give him money, they would die and go to hell. The villagers, being naïve and scared, would denounce the experience and give him all their money in order to "save" themselves. He used the money to support his drug and alcohol addictions.

One of our team members was new to warfare prayer. He began to pray that all the curses this priest had placed on the villagers would fall back on the priest's own head to his own destruction. Granted, this priest was an evil person, but as intercessors our job is to pray for mercy for any individual being used by evil and to pray against the spirits operating behind the scenes. I was team leader so it was my responsibility to handle this situation. I corrected this new, zealous warrior and explained that we pray against spirits, not individuals. I then redirected the prayers of the group in the proper fashion. We addressed the spirits operating behind the priest and the region and asked God to reveal Himself to this man and bring him to salvation.

11. Perform prophetic acts.

Barbara Wentroble defines a prophetic act as "a thing or deed done, having the powers of a prophet, an action or decree that foreshadows."[1] A scriptural example is the battle of Jericho, recorded in Joshua 6:3–5:

> "You shall march around the city, all the men of war circling the city once. You shall do so for six days. Also seven priests shall carry seven trumpets of rams' horns before the ark; then on the seventh day you shall march around the city seven times, and the priests shall blow the trumpets. It shall be that when they make a long blast with the ram's horn, and when you hear the sound of the trumpet, all the people shall shout with a great shout; and the wall of the city will fall down flat, and the people will go up every man straight ahead."
>
> NASB

Please be discreet when performing prophetic acts. Try not to draw attention to yourself or do something that will put the safety of the team in jeopardy. Do not destroy historic relics or property of a temple. Not only does this put

Christians in a bad light, but it could get you and the team thrown into jail.

12. Speak prophetic proclamations.
A prophetic proclamation is an announcement or decree given with the authority of a prophet. The above-mentioned confrontation of Isis is an example of prophetic proclamation toward a demonic entity. An example found in Scripture is 2 Timothy 4:17:

> But the Lord stood with me and strengthened me, so that through me the proclamation might be fully accomplished, and that all the Gentiles might hear; and I was rescued out of the lion's mouth.
>
> NASB

I was teaching a group of intercessors in the town of La Junta, Colorado. They had asked if I would be willing to join them in prayer on the property owned by one of the intercessors and I had agreed. On that ranch is a hill. This hill is the meeting point of three counties in Colorado and is the high point of all three counties. Individuals involved in the New Age movement and meditation travel to high places such as this to pray and seek spiritual enlightenment.

After the couple purchased the property they began to receive phone calls from people asking to climb the hill. They gladly allowed these strangers access with no knowledge of what was occurring once they reached the top. Once they became aware of spiritual warfare, these landowners surmised that demonic and witchcraft practices had occurred there. They knew they needed to climb the hill and pray, but they wanted someone with spiritual warfare experience to pray with them. A group of intercessors from their church, the pastor, his family and I climbed the hill.

Landowners have legal authority to confront demonic activity on their land. The intercessors had already prepared spiritually for this mission. The Lord had directed one couple to bring stakes with Scripture written on them. It was obvious what we were to do.

Upon reaching the top we discovered three altars. They were built of rocks and were in the formation of a triangle. One of the rock altars contained the bones of an animal. It was obvious that we needed to pray and destroy these demonic altars. God directed us to perform several prophetic acts. First we threw all the rocks down the hill; then we threw down the animal bones. We declared that the demonic powers of these altars were broken off the land. As we continued to pray and read Scripture, God began to impress upon us to perform another prophetic act and to make a prophetic declaration.

Colorado was in a severe drought at this time. It was especially bad in this area of the state; all of the vegetation was dead. From the top of this hill as far as the eye could see was dead grass. Four of the team members were impressed by the Lord to perform a prophetic act to declare the drought broken. We divided the team into three groups. Each group stood on a location where the rock altars had been built. We anointed each site with oil and poured water on the ground at the center of the triangle. After we poured the water, we drove the stakes with Scripture written on them into the ground.

The pastor, who has spiritual authority in this region, declared prophetically that the drought would be broken in that region and on the land. Then I declared that the grass would begin to turn green, that life would return to the land, and that the people of the region would see the green grass and life on the land and give God the glory. Within a month, four inches of rain had fallen. As you approached the property line of the ranch, the grass was noticeably greener than that of the surrounding land.

13. Pray until there is breakthrough or your assignment is complete.

As intercessors we need to be able to discern when breakthrough has occurred. The following are a few examples of how a team might perceive spiritual breakthrough.

You will experience a sudden shift from warfare prayer to peace, or a shift from crying and travail to peace.

You will discern the breakthrough in the spiritual realm.

God will speak that there is breakthrough.

You will know that your agenda at that location is complete.

There will be a sudden drastic change in the weather as breakthrough occurs. I have been with many teams on location when the weather changed as we prayed and broke the power of the enemy over the region. It is an awesome experience. Here is an example of one such instance.

It was near the end of a six-day trip in Egypt. Before and throughout the trip, the Lord had given our team of six members many Scriptures concerning rain, water and clouds. Here are three of them:

"See, the LORD rides on a swift cloud and is coming to Egypt. The idols of Egypt tremble before him, and the hearts of the Egyptians melt within them" (Isaiah 19:1).

"You heavens above, rain down righteousness; let the clouds shower it down. Let the earth open wide, let salvation spring up, let righteousness grow with it; I, the LORD, have created it" (Isaiah 45:8).

"For I will pour water on the thirsty land, and streams on the dry ground" (Isaiah 44:3).

As we researched the topic of Egypt, we soon realized that we would be dealing with its roots of Freemasonry. One of the team members, whom I will call "Paul," had been a 33rd degree Mason, as had his father before him. When Paul discovered the truth about Freemasonry, he denounced his connection with it, broke all ties with it and threw out anything he owned that was related to it. The Lord told us that Paul would be the point man of the trip. God was going to use him powerfully.

We scheduled a day to visit the ruins of a temple. It was built by the pharaoh whom we believed to have been one of the initiators of Masonic practices. We knew that all of the idol and icon worship perpetuated during his reign would be represented there. Paul was in intercession all night and all day before arriving at this location. Alice and I knew that something strategic would occur on this site.

When we arrived we learned that the site was closed because of excavations. Gigi, our guide, was a Christian on fire for God. She got out of the van to convince the workers to let us in.

I need to pause and mention a bit of background information here. Because I have the same skin and hair coloring of Egyptian women, many people thought I was Egyptian. (On this trip I actually received three marriage proposals; one man offered Alice a thousand camels for me!) Well, at this location my "new identity" came in handy. We could see that Gigi was having a difficult time. So Alice instructed me to sit in the front seat of the van, take off my sunglasses and smile at the men overseeing the entrance to the site. It worked! We hid our amusement as they ushered us in.

When we entered the ruins we were astonished. All around us stood large obelisks and on each of these obelisks were hieroglyphics. These hieroglyphics included the Masonic symbols that we see today. We went to the entrance gate of the temple and began to pray. Gigi told us to pray quickly because she was not going to be able to stall the workers much longer.

Paul prayed prayers of identificational repentance and denounced Freemasonry as a demonic secret society. Alice then instructed him to break the power of Freemasonry off the land and to cut its power to the other nations where it had spread. As soon as Paul broke the power of Freemasonry, it began instantly to rain. We were excited and several of us began to weep. Gigi then instructed us to leave quickly because the workers were losing patience. We promptly obliged.

Once on the van she asked, "Do you understand the miracle we are in?"

We replied, "Yes, the Lord told us He would come in the clouds, rain and water and He did."

Gigi then told us, "I am thirty-three years old; I was born and raised in Egypt. This is the month of October, which is considered the dry season. I have never in my life seen it rain in Egypt in the dry season. This has never happened." We were all floored.

Well, not only did it rain, it rained a lot! It was a Houston, Texas, kind of rain. It lasted four hours with strong gusty winds. That night at dinner, the hotel and restaurant staff were standing at the windows watching it rain. They did not know what to think.

As we left the restaurant that evening, the manager was standing by the door watching it rain. We asked what he thought about it. His answer proved to us that God can use anyone to confirm His plans. This man did not know who we were and had not met us, but he looked right at us and responded, "It is because you are here that it rained." Speechless, all six of us turned the corner to leave the restaurant and immediately began once again to weep.

The final amount of the rainfall was one and three-fourths inches. The normal *annual* rainfall in that part of the world is one inch. God can and will manifest in the natural realm breakthrough that has occurred in the spiritual realm. Isn't He an awesome and miraculous God?

14. Release God's purposes on the land.

This is sometimes called *replacement*, meaning you pray and release the opposite of the enemy's plan on the land. Here are a few illustrations of how to do this.

If death is present you speak life over the region.

If fear is the issue you are dealing with, you speak boldness, power, love and a sound mind.

If pride is confronting you, you speak humility and a contrite spirit.

If witchcraft is in operation, you speak freedom and a submissive spirit to God.

If racism or prejudice is evident, you speak love and acceptance.

15. Pray that the redemptive gift of the land be restored.

The redemptive gift is God's original purpose for the land before poor stewardship and the enemy's plans stole that purpose. John Dawson explains this further in his book *Taking Our Cities for God*:

> I believe God intends the city to be a place of shelter, a place of communion and a place of personal liberation as its citizens practice a division of labor according to their unique gifts. I believe our cities have the mark of God's sovereign purpose on them. Our cities contain what I call a redemptive gift.[2]

Greg and I lived in Houston for ten years. It is the medical hub of Texas; some of the leading doctors in the world work in the medical center downtown. This city is also a melting pot for many nations. People from numerous countries and ethnicities live here. Many believe that this city has a redemptive gift of healing and also has been blessed with an anointing to bring healing to the nations.

16. Ask the Lord for salvation of lost souls.

Pray boldly. Remember that this is the ultimate goal of spiritual warfare.

17. Thank the Lord for the victory.

Remember that God is the one who receives credit for the victory. We are only vessels that He chooses to allow to partner with Him in intercession. David is a good example for us to follow upon the defeat of Goliath and the Philistines in 1 Samuel 17:45–47:

> David said to the Philistine, "You come against me with sword and spear and javelin, but I come against you in the name of the LORD Almighty, the God of the armies of Israel, whom you have defied. This day the LORD will hand you over to me, and I'll strike you down and cut off your head. Today I will give the carcasses of the Philistine army to the birds of the air and the beasts of the earth, and the whole world will know that there is a God in Israel."

David did not take credit for the victory; notice he stated the Lord was giving the Philistines into his hands.

18. Continue with praise and worship.
Worship the Lord and praise Him. Worship is one of the most powerful weapons of war. Examples abound in Scripture. Here is one:

> After consulting the people, Jehoshaphat appointed men to sing to the LORD and to praise him for the splendor of his holiness as they went out at the head of the army, saying:
> "Give thanks to the LORD, for his love endures forever." As they began to sing and praise, the LORD set ambushes against the men of Ammon and Moab and Mount Seir who were invading Judah, and they were defeated.
>
> 2 Chronicles 20:21–22

19. And finally, be expectant.
Pray with fervency, expectancy and faith. He who has called you is faithful to fulfill His promises.

Exploring the Essentials

1. Do you have a story to share of effective on-site prayer?
2. Explain a time when you prayed out of obedience rather than feelings.
3. In warfare prayer we pray against territorial spirits, not individuals. Why is this?
4. Have you been present when an intercessor or group prayed against an individual? If you have been involved in this practice, ask the Lord to forgive you. Pray that the enemy's schemes would be defeated in this individual's life and that the Lord would begin to soften and move in this person's heart.
5. Have you ever been involved in a prophetic act? What were the results?
6. Have you made prophetic proclamations over a person, situation or city? What happened as a result of the proclamation?
7. What do you see as the redemptive gift of your city?

9

Counterattack

WHEN WE BEGIN to advance in our God-given authority and wage war against the schemes of the enemy, we will experience counterattack. A counterattack is a reprisal, one attack made in response to another. In the spiritual realm this opposing action is an effort to thwart the breakthrough achieved through spiritual warfare.

Types of Counterattacks

If you are in a situation when issues begin to arise that are difficult to surmount, contact your supporting intercessors and ask them to increase the prayer coverage. It is critically important for the team members to make right choices in the face of counterattack. Remember Satan is the father of lies; he and his minions do not speak truth.

Here are several counterattacks that your team may face.

Discouragement and Distraction

As the team moves forward in the prayer agenda, it is usually attacked through discouragement and distraction. Discouragement can affect either individuals or teams. It works against you personally like this. As you pray, thoughts will begin to flood your mind such as, *That was a terrible prayer. I am off; that was not anointed.* When this begins to happen, do not stop praying. As a matter of fact, do not focus on it or acknowledge it. This is an attempt to stop your prayers. Keep your focus on God and do not allow this to deter you.

Prayer journeys can be mentally, emotionally, physically and spiritually draining. As the trip moves forward and the team gets tired, discouragement will try to take a foothold. Days where things have not gone smoothly and strong resistance has been experienced might also be an opening for the team to grow discouraged. Thoughts and feelings of questioning the assignment might begin to surface. At this point it is time to regroup. A team prayer meeting and worship time will build faith and direct the focus back to the Lord and the assignment at hand. The team leader should encourage the team and impart faith to move forward.

Distractions are also not uncommon. While on the prayer journey to Egypt (this was the same day that I almost walked into the circle of machine guns) we had what we termed later as a "Maria day." We asked Maria, our guide, to take us to the oldest city in that part of Egypt. We wanted to pray at the ancient gateway of that area of the nation. She said that she knew exactly where we wanted to go and would take us there.

The day turned out to be a disaster. Maria was a Coptic Christian and the bishop of the Coptic Christian Churches of Egypt lived in that area. She took us to his church and told us that we needed to be there. She then asked if we wanted to meet the bishop; we said we had other plans. Maria begged us to do this for her because she had wanted to meet this bishop her whole life.

We waited an hour for her to have a meeting with this bishop who spoke no English. While he and Maria conversed, a priest who was visiting the bishop that day entered the room. He needed a ride back to his village, and Maria quickly volunteered to take him. We spent the next two hours transporting the priest back to his village and the whole day was lost.

The team fought discouragement and frustration because we never made it to the ancient gateway. But we did not get angry; we did not gripe. We regrouped that night, focused on God and set our sights on the prayer agenda for the next day. Needless to say, however, we did not request Maria as our guide again. We employed a new guide who would take us to the locations we desired.

Competition, Jealousy, Accusation

"I love the gift of intercession and praying with intercessors," the woman told me, "because it is great competition! I am competitive and I love to receive the word of the Lord before anybody else. Come on, Becca! You're competitive, too. I am sure that is why you pray and intercede. You want to be the first to receive the word of the Lord!"

I am sure some of you are shocked to read this quote. Not as surprised, shocked and grieved as I was when it was said to me by another intercessor. Guard your heart against competition while in warfare prayer. Bless others as you pray and pray in agreement with the team members. I had to correct this intercessor and explain that competition is not our motivation.

Jealousy among team members is detrimental to any mission. It is usually the result of a competitive spirit or when an individual desires recognition. The enemy will try frequently to stir up jealousy. Do not go there! I have observed this spirit in operation many times and it not only brings harm to the individual who has embraced it but also to other team members. I have seen this spirit adversely affect not only prayer initiatives but also ministries.

If you feel jealousy begin to surface while on a prayer journey, do not stop the team and ask them to pray for you. This distracts the team from the prayer assignment and places the focus on the enemy. Pray in the opposite spirit by asking God to bless and give increased anointing to the other intercessors. In your own time with the Lord later repent of those thoughts and audibly rebuke a spirit of jealousy. Remember demons cannot read your thoughts; when addressing one, speak out loud with authority!

Accusation is another tool the enemy uses to distract intercessors from their prayer agenda. The enemy and his cohorts will speak lies to the intercessors concerning other team members and team leadership. Do not entertain these thoughts and do not share them with other team members. Voicing these thoughts opens a door for gossip and rebellion against authority.

Have you ever gone to a restaurant, ordered a meal, received your dinner plate and realized it was the wrong dish? You did not order that meal. You do not want it. You return it. The same is true when dealing with a spirit of accusation. There is camaraderie among the team members. It is a strife-free environment. Then suddenly one of the intercessors begins to experience negative thoughts, lies and accusations concerning the other team associates and team leadership. The intercessor did not order these thoughts or want them! Do as stated above: Pray in the exact opposite spirit of this accusatory foe. If necessary step aside and in a low whisper state, "I command the spirit of accusation to leave, I will not submit to you." Then rejoin the group.

Disunity

Paul writes in 1 Corinthians 1:10:

I appeal to you, brothers, in the name of our Lord Jesus Christ, that all of you agree with one another so that there may be no divisions among you and that you may be perfectly united in mind and thought.

Many attitudes and actions can bring division to a warfare prayer initiative, but if disunity becomes an issue then you might as well pack your bags and go home! No battalion advancing into battle will succeed if the soldiers are bickering among themselves and not focused together on the task at hand. On a warfare prayer initiative you have to be alert and a team player. Remember the discussion on unity in chapter 4. The team has signed a covenant; choose to walk in unity.

The Lure of Defiled Plunder

The sin of Achan and the consequences of that sin are described in Joshua 7. We learn a great truth about warfare through this incident. When the Israelites destroyed Jericho, Achan took plunder for his personal gain. It resulted in the Israelites' defeat at Ai and the death of Achan and his sons.

When engaging in warfare prayer never take anything from the land. I have seen team members attempt to take rocks or some token from the territory as a reminder of the battle and victory. This opens the door for the enemy to attack. Demons can attach themselves to inanimate objects. If something is removed from the land where warfare occurred, then the demons that were evicted from the land will attempt to attach themselves to the object.

Also, never take home an object that has a territorial spirit or demon god or goddess depicted on it. These objects symbolize demonic practices or idol worship. We must keep our homes spiritually clean. These items are a major open door for counterattack upon returning home from the prayer initiative.

Retaliation on Home Territory

Not only will counterattacks occur while on the battlefield, they will also take place back home. Even though victory in battle was won, the enemy has not forgotten his defeat. He will want to oppose the plan of God and continue to harass those who have brought humiliation and destruction to his ranks. Barbara Wentroble explains backlash in *Prophetic Intercession*:

> The enemy does not stop his maneuvers to interfere with the will of God just because we have experienced a victory. He is stubborn in his pursuit to stop the plan of God. Therefore, he engages in an activity often referred to as backlash. One of Webster's definitions for "backlash" is "a quick, sharp recoil."
>
> Considering the fact that the enemy is likened to a serpent or snake, we can understand this definition. A serpent will recoil and try to strike a target he considers his enemy. Satan does the same thing in spiritual warfare. Many times in spiritual battle, he will recoil and try to strike again after God's people have secured a victory.[1]

It is extremely vital that the supportive intercessors continue to cover the team and family members for at least four weeks following a warfare prayer initiative. Also, the team members should continue to spend quality time in the Lord's presence following a time of spiritual warfare. Guard your heart against pride. Give God the glory for the victory. We are His vessels; He is the one who allowed the victory to be achieved.

Glorifying the Enemy

One final word on the subject of counterattacks, and that is not to talk excessively about them. It is perfectly acceptable to share information about counterattacks with other intercessors in order to increase prayer coverage. It is not acceptable, however, to talk continually about the backlash of the enemy.

Matthew 12:34 states, "For out of the overflow of the heart the mouth speaks." I have participated on teams where the enemy's attempts to thwart victory were discussed more than the plan of the Lord. Why do we focus on darkness instead of on God? We are called to glorify God, not the wiles of spirits of darkness. By concentrating on Satan's attempts to foil the victory, we are glorifying him, not God. Not only is our focus off balance, but this also opens a door for further retaliations. I choose to praise the King of kings and the Lord of lords! He is the One truly worthy of all praise.

Exploring the Essentials

1. Has there been a time when the enemy brought counterattack in your life? What happened? How did you stand?
2. Do you struggle with distraction, discouragement or jealousy? Repent for these issues. Ask God to bring breakthrough.
3. Share a time when you overcame discouragement. Thank the Lord for the victory He gave you in this situation.
4. Share a time when you overcame competition and jealousy. Thank the Lord for the victory in this situation. If you still struggle with these thoughts, repent and ask God to give you breakthrough.
5. How do we stand against accusation?
6. Discuss a time when you stood successfully against a spirit of accusation.
7. Do you have an item or items in your home that can be considered defiled plunder? If so, break ties with the object and throw it away!
8. How do we guard against glorifying the enemy?

10

Breakthrough!

YOU HAVE COMPLETED your mission: Expect to see breakthrough!

I have mentioned the word *breakthrough* throughout the book but have not given a specific definition. Webster's dictionary tells us that *breakthrough* means an offensive thrust that penetrates a defensive line in warfare, a sudden and strikingly important advance against resistance. When successful strategic-level spiritual warfare has transpired, reports of breakthrough—the stunning and encouraging evidence of the battles won in the heavenlies—will begin to emerge. In *The Breaker Anointing* Barbara Yoder explains the widespread effects of breakthrough:

> It is an anointing that affects individuals, churches, and cities. When the breaker anointing comes into an area it results in changes not only in individuals but also in churches, the socio-political structure, and the belief systems of the city.[1]

Micah 2:13 says, "One who breaks open the way will go up before them; they will break through the gate and go out. Their king will pass through before them, the LORD at their head." It is awe-inspiring and exciting to watch as the Lord goes forth into a region and lives are transformed.

This Is Breakthrough!

Many times as we proceed into strategic-level warfare prayer, breakthrough will manifest itself immediately as we pray. Other times it will come later. In either case, revival, change and salvation will begin to spring forth.

I have shared many stories of breakthrough throughout the previous chapters. I would like to close with three more stories that show different aspects of breakthrough.

A Serial Killer Caught

A serial killer was on the loose in the city of Houston. He had murdered four individuals and the police had no leads. Spirits of fear and death were beginning to grip the city.

During a prayer meeting at church one night, we focused on the capture of the serial killer. We began to pray that the police would be led supernaturally to the killer. We prayed that fear and death would not have access to the city. We declared that this terrorizing would come to an end and that he would be caught *that evening*.

When I arrived home, I quickly turned on the television to hear the breaking news at the top of the hour. I heard the announcer state that the police had received a phone call leading them to the killer and that he had been arrested. The call to the police came during the exact hour that we had been praying. This is breakthrough!

Russia Maintains Freedom of Religion

I have mentioned several times the prayer journey into Russia. We advanced forward at a strategic time. The Russian Orthodox Church considers itself the only true religion to assure salvation. The bishop of the entire Russian Orthodox Church was in the process of convincing Russia's President Putin to ban all other religions and to pass a law making it illegal to attend any other church.

On many of the locations where we prayed the Lord birthed in us the prophetic declaration, "Freedom!" We were obedient and decreed this over the land. During the time we were there praying, several other teams were also in Russia engaging in warfare prayer. Several weeks after returning home, President Bush spoke with President Putin and convinced him not to pass this law. Russia still has significant progress to make concerning religious freedom, but non-Orthodox religions are legally permitted to worship in Russia today. Freedom of religion is still present in Russia. This is breakthrough!

The Pope Asks Pardon for Violence

Remember the story of Santa Maria Maggiore in chapter 2? The bloodshed of Jewish men and women during the Crusades and the Holocaust was part of the focus of our prayers on this trip to Rome. About five months after we returned home, Greg was watching the news when he called for me to come quickly. As I approached the television, I saw that Pope John Paul was speaking. He was repenting and asking pardon for the use of violence and for the attitudes of mistrust and opposition toward followers of other religions, including the Jewish race. He even asked the Lord for mercy for these sins. By doing this, the pope was defying Roman Catholic dogma concerning the infallibility of a pope, as he identified himself with the harmful decisions and actions of former popes. This is breakthrough!

Accepting the Call

Speaking through the prophet Hosea, the Lord declares, "My people are destroyed from lack of knowledge" (Hosea 4:6). Throughout the world men, women and children are trapped in spiritual darkness. As the Church and Bride of Christ, we are being called by God to advance, engage in war, claim the land and set the captives free. Yes, we are the Bride and Christ is the Bridegroom. How humiliating for Satan to see an imperfect Bride partnering with God to defeat evil strongholds over territories!

"Behold, I give unto you power to tread on serpents and scorpions, and over all the power of the enemy: and nothing shall by any means hurt you" (Luke 10:19, KJV). Jesus has called us to walk in our God-given authority to tread upon principalities and powers. Psalm 44:5 decrees, "Through thee will we push down our enemies: through thy name will we tread them under that rise up against us" (KJV). Jesus died on the cross to bring salvation to a dying world and to defeat Satan's attempts to claim the earth as his own. It is in Jesus' name that we move ahead to defeat all forms of darkness and demonic entities. It is in His name that we tread on serpents and scorpions.

Perhaps God is calling you to pray for your neighborhood. Maybe you are being directed to pray for your city. Some of you are called to the nations. Let's accept the call to strategic-level spiritual warfare prayer. Let's press forward, take the land and triumph in victory. Let's go in the assurance that we do have the authority to tread.

Exploring the Essentials

1. Describe a time when you were involved with break-through that ushered change into an individual's life, a situation, your church, your neighborhood, city, state

or a nation. Thank the Lord for the breakthrough and transformation.

2. Join in praying this closing prayer:

Father, I thank You for Your faithfulness toward me, the peoples and the lands of the earth. Thank You for calling me into a partnership of intercession. It is an honor and privilege to carry the burdens and prayer assignments You have appointed for me. Father, I ask that You reveal the territories You have allocated to me. Speak the prayer agenda You have for me. Father, give me ears to hear and eyes to see what You are saying to me in this season. Give me Your heart for my neighborhood, city, state and nation. Lord, I cry out for the nations of the earth. I declare that all the schemes of the enemy will be exposed, plundered and destroyed. Lord, I profess that I accept Your plan for my life and my territory. Speak to me and I will move forward in obedience. Lord, help me to remain pure before You. Keep me from temptation and help me lead a life of holiness. I am expectant that You will speak. Thank You for the privilege of moving forward. I give You all the honor, glory and praise. In Jesus' name. Amen.

Pastoral/Church Covenant
for Prayer Journey Participants

A member of your congregation, _____
_____, has requested to be a participant on a prayer
journey to _____.
The church or ministry coordinating the trip is: _____
_____. The contact person is: _____
_____.

The participants are being sponsored by churches, personal
funds and different parachurch ministries.

As part of the training and equipping for the prayer journey,
each participant is being asked to provide a recommendation
from his or her pastor or spiritual advisor. Prayer journeys
involve strategic-level warfare and it is important that the
participating intercessors have appropriate spiritual covering.
This referral assures the team leadership that this participant
is under the authority of a pastor. Each participant is also

required to mobilize local prayer coverage. We are requesting that the supporting church also join in providing the intercessor with a prayer cover.

Your church or ministry and staff are released from any and all liability for accidents, sickness or death of the participant during the trip.

Pastoral Reference Information

I am aware that _____
has applied for participation in a prayer journey to _____
_____. I have known this individual for
_____ years. I find that this person's character, maturity
and life circumstances are such that I can recommend him/her
for participation in a prayer journey. I will covenant to cover
him/her in prayer during the prayer journey.

(If you are unable to recommend this individual, an attachment with an explanation would be appreciated.)

Pastor's name: _____

Church name: _____

City and State: _____ Zip: _____

Phone: (____) _____
Fax: (____) _____

Email: _____

Pastor's signature: _____

Date: _____

Note: This form is for suggested use only and is not intended to be a legal document. If you have any legal questions, consult an attorney.

Adapted from *Intercessors and Pastors* by Eddie and Alice Smith (Houston: SpiriTruth Publishing, 2000), 168. Used by permission. Available at www.prayerbookstore.com.

B

Team Covenant
for Prayer Journey Participants

We commit to serve Christ together for a special season of intercessory labor. We desire, personally and corporately, to uphold the following values throughout this endeavor:

- To honor each other, remembering that God has created each of us differently and given each of us differing gifts according to His purposes.
- To bring unity to the team through taking time to be with the Lord to renew ourselves, supporting and ministering to each other, enjoying each other, resolving all personal differences and forgiving each other as He has forgiven us, so as not to give Satan a foothold.

- To submit to the authority of our leader whom God has appointed over us.
- To strive to be faithful to the task by preparing ourselves spiritually, mentally and physically; by pursuing an attitude of servanthood to the people of the land over which we will pray and to each other; and by striving to be faithful servants, as God directs, during this time and in the future.
- To remember that our primary purpose is lost souls and the Kingdom of God. "The Lord is not slow in keeping his promise, as some understand slowness. He is patient with you, not wanting anyone to perish, but everyone to come to repentance" (2 Peter 3:9).

Date signed: _____

Team members' names and signatures:

1. _____

2. _____

3. _____

4. _____

5. _____

6. _____

7. _____

8. _____

9. (Additional lines as needed.)

Liability Clause

By signing below I signify that I assume personal responsibility and liability for any injury, loss or inconvenience that happens to me while participating in the prayer journey to _____.
I do not hold the ministries in charge of the prayer journey, the staff, the team leadership, my pastor or my church responsible for any harm that may come to me on the trip.

Date signed: _____   _____

Team Member's Printed Name and Signature:

_____

Note: This form is for suggested use only and is not intended to be a legal document. If you have any legal questions, consult an attorney.

Adapted from *Intercessors and Pastors* by Eddie and Alice Smith (Houston: SpiriTruth Publishing, 2000), 169. Used by permission. Available at www.prayerbookstore.com.

C

Personal Information Form
for Prayer Journey Participants

Date: _____ Deadline to return this form: _____

Please print your name below, as it appears on your passport.

Name: _____
(last, first, middle)

Informal name: _____

Title (please circle): Mr. Mrs. Ms. Miss Rev. Dr.

Home address: _____

City: _____ State: ___ Zip: _____

Home phone: (___) _____

Work phone: (___) _____

Occupation: _____

SSN: ____/___/____ Sex: ☐ M ☐ F

Country of citizenship: _____
Passport #: _____
Expiration date: _____/_____/_____

Family Information

Marital status (please circle): Single Engaged Married
Divorced Separated
Spouse's name: _____
Children's names and ages:

_____

_____

_____

_____

Health/Insurance

Do you consider your health ☐ good ☐ average or
☐ poor?
Please describe any physical disability: _____

_____

Would this disability present physical limitations that might
hinder your involvement in the prayer journey? _____ How?

_____

Are you currently taking prescription medications? _____
If yes, please explain.

_____

_____

Are you allergic to any medications? _____ If yes, which ones:

_____

Do you have any other allergies? _____ If yes, which ones:

_____

Do you have health insurance coverage? _____

Company: _____

Phone: _____ Policy number:_____

Does your insurance cover emergencies overseas? _____

Emergency Contact

Name: _____ Relationship: _____

Address: _____

City: _____ State: ___ Zip: _____

Phone: (___)_____

Email: _____

Spiritual Background

Briefly describe when and how you came to know Christ personally.

_____

_____

_____

_____

How would you describe your relationship with the Lord in the past year?

☐ Stagnant ☐ Wilderness ☐ Learning time

☐ Growing ☐ Intimate ☐ Excellent

Describe your involvement in your church or ministry activities in the past.

_____

_____

_____

_____

_____

Check any of the following areas you *presently* struggle with or feel the enemy *might* have established as a possible stronghold in your life.

☐ procrastination	☐ laziness	☐ fear(s)	☐ unbelief
☐ lying	☐ prejudice	☐ lust	☐ phobias
☐ rage	☐ control	☐ adultery	☐ rebellion
☐ pornography	☐ moodiness	☐ anxiety	☐ chronic fatigue
☐ pride	☐ chronic sickness	☐ critical spirit	☐ self-pity
☐ rejection	☐ anger	☐ worthlessness	☐ addiction
☐ jealousy	☐ nightmares		

Ministry involvement (check all that apply to you):

____ I know how to lead someone to Christ.

____ I have been on a deliverance team.

____ I have been on a spiritual warfare prayer journey(s). Please describe where and when:

_____

_____

_____

_____

____ I have been on a mission trip(s). Please describe where and when: _____

_____

_____

_____

_____

☐ I have been trained in intercessory prayer.

☐ I am involved in weekly Bible study or prayer group.

Write down your ministry strengths, spiritual gifts or skills that might be helpful on a prayer journey. (Does the Lord use you, for instance, in performing miracles, singing, playing an instrument, discerning, healing, evangelism, showing mercy?)

_____

_____

_____

_____

_____

Why do you want to be a part of a prayer journey?

_____

_____

_____

Describe your level of experience in the area of warfare prayer. What about intercessory prayer? What training have you received?

_____

_____

_____

_____

Describe your cross-cultural experience. Have you traveled overseas and visited other cultures?

_____

_____

_____

_____

_____

What books on prayer have you read in the last five years?

_____

_____

_____

_____

What books on spiritual warfare or spiritual mapping have you read in the last five years?

_____

_____

_____

_____

_____

_____

Explain your concept of spiritual warfare. What are your views on demonic strongholds? What authority do you believe Christians have to displace them?

_____

_____

_____

_____

_____

Briefly describe an experience you had with spiritual warfare. Were you victorious?

_____

_____

_____

_____

_____

Relational

Do you see yourself as a team player? _____ If no, why not?

_____

_____

_____

_____

Explain any difficulties you have with other Christians whose doctrinal viewpoints differ from your own.

_____

_____

_____

_____

Is it difficult for you to follow directions? _____ If yes, explain why.

_____

_____

Would you follow the leadership of a woman?_____

If the team travels, you would be expected to stay with the team. There will be no individual travel allowed, such as visiting friends, other ministries, tours. Can you accept this policy without reservation? ☐ yes ☐ no

Signature: _____ Date: _____

Note: This form is for suggested use only and is not intended to be a legal document. If you have any legal questions, consult an attorney.

Adapted from *Intercessors and Pastors* by Eddie and Alice Smith (Houston: SpiriTruth Publishing, 2000), 170–172. Used by permission. Available at www.prayerbookstore.com.

D

Russia/Ukraine Prayer Journey Report

THE FOLLOWING IS a report on the Russia/Ukraine warfare prayer journey that I led in September 2001. I have included this in the book as an example of how to document a prayer journey. It is good to produce a report such as this as soon as possible after returning from the trip. This will help you keep the facts straight in your mind, particularly if you are preparing a report for your pastor or a sponsoring ministry.

Prayer Journey Report
Russia/Ukraine 2001
Team Leader Becca Greenwood

This prayer journey team consisted of nine members: Becca Greenwood, 34; Greg Greenwood, 35; Nan Grys, 55; Jonathan Davis, 27; Chad Chmelar, 26; Patsy Chmelar, 53; Darla Ryden, 39; Venetia Nelms, 39; Chris Walden, 29.

These team members were selected based on our long-term relationships, spiritual depth and prayer. Also, a couple of the team members asked to come so they could be trained in spiritual warfare. I felt that the team was incredible. There was great unity and I would gladly take any of the journeyers with me again.

Research Information

When we began our research it became obvious that the Lord was directing us to pray in Novgorod, Russia, and Kiev, Ukraine. These two cities are the oldest cities in Russian history. They carry great weight and significance in the history of Russia and Ukraine and they have strong spiritual connections.

The earliest peoples of Russia, the Slavs, Scythians and Trypillians inhabited these areas and were steeped in pagan and occult practices. They worshiped Volos, Perun, Mokosha, Svarog, Divanna, Kupala, Sophia and Zeus as well as many other minor gods and goddesses. These tribal groups performed human sacrifices to these gods and goddesses on a regular basis. Many children were kidnapped from other tribal groups and forcefully and brutally sacrificed to the gods. The children of all tribes were told throughout childhood that if they were not obedient they would be taken to Zeus.

The oldest tribal group that the Lord brought to our attention was the Trypillian culture. It is believed that they inhabited the geographic area now known as Ukraine four thousand years ago; some books stated seven thousand years. Their whole existence was intertwined with the worship of the "Great Moist Mother Earth." She was also worshiped under the names Kupala and Divanna, better known as Diana. The Dnieper, the Don and the Danube are rivers in Ukraine and Russia that are named after this goddess.

We dealt with her in Ukraine; the places she was worshiped are well documented. One of these is a mount called the Devich Mount where only maidens were allowed. During the month of September, a priestess and nine maidens would climb the mount and perform rituals and sacrifices to Divanna. A form of the goddess was in the center and surrounding her were nine niches in which each maiden would simultaneously perform their worship to this goddess. Our team consisted of nine members, which God used as a prophetic sign. I will tell more of this when I share about praying in Kiev. Many of the pagan worship forms involved blood sacrifice. Zeus worship also occurred in this area.

On this mountain at birth, each female was assigned a patron goddess. As a result the women in the home were worshiped by the men as deities. We discovered there a New Age group under the leadership of a man named Oles Berdnyk. The name of this group is the Ukrainian Spiritual Republic. They are worshiping on this mount and trying to reinstate worship of this goddess and all her ancient worship practices. They are petitioning individuals from around the world with Slavic blood to come and find the spiritual enlightenment of the ancestors. They hold three tours a year and take individuals to the most "sacred" of spiritual locations for enlightenment under the worship of the "Great Moist Mother Earth"—Divanna.

In the ninth century, these tribal people stated that there was no order or rule in their land and asked a Viking, Rurik, to come and rule. He accepted. He is an ancestor of Vladimir, who is the famous ruler known for "Christianizing" Russia through forced baptism. The Vikings worshiped all of the gods and goddesses that were established in this land and also brought a few of their own. Vladimir worshiped all of these gods and goddesses and participated in the practice of sacrificing humans. He was especially involved in the worship of Perun and Mokosha.

In the year A.D. 988 Vladimir decided to accept baptism into the Orthodox Church. This decision was made for political reasons. He desired to marry a Byzantine princess and the royal family would agree only if Vladimir accepted baptism into Orthodoxy. This also produced peaceful relationships between the two empires.

After his marriage, Vladimir demanded that all the citizens of Kiev and Novgorod be baptized. If citizens refused, he burned their homes and possessions. If this did not work, he killed them. In Novgorod, the Volga River was full of blood and dead bodies. The Volga is half a mile in width and it is told that one could walk across the width of the river on dead bodies. Unfortunately, we did not receive the full extent of this information until we were in Kiev. We assume that this never was discovered in our research because Orthodox priests wrote much of the early history of Novgorod and Kiev, and they knew that this forced baptism portrays the church in a negative light.

We did feel that there was an issue with the water while in Novgorod. We prayed at the river and poured anointing oil in the Volga asking God to purify the water of bloodshed and defilement. We did this without knowledge of the tremendous deaths associated with the river.

Vladimir destroyed all the pagan idols, but the people simply replaced their gods with biblical prophets and saints. Perun became Elijah, for instance, Mokosha became Mary/Sophia, Volos became St. Blaise. Also, the Russians did not want to be subject to the authority of the Greek Orthodox Church, so they changed the doctrine slightly to form their own religion. The result was the formation of the Russian Orthodox Church.

Novgorod

Before beginning the prayer journey to Novgorod and Kiev, the team attended a conference called Gideon's Army II, hosted by Global Harvest Ministries. The focus of this conference was spiritual breakthrough for the European nations in the 40/70 window.

One of the team intercessors received direction before we departed for Germany. The Lord had her purchase keys, anointing oil and mustard seeds for the team. As God directed, we were to plant our keys in strategic locations. These keys were to be anointed with oil and buried with mustard seeds. This was to be done as a prophetic act decreeing that God was unlocking Russia and Ukraine with His anointing and that as a result a harvest of souls would begin to come forth. In the last service of Gideon's Army II, one of the Intercessory leaders spoke a prophetic word over the prayer journey teams that were attending: "God has given you the keys to unlock His purposes in the 40/70 window." This word was confirmation that we were on the right track and we would see breakthrough as a result of our prayers.

After leaving Gideon's Army II, we flew to St. Petersburg and spent the night before departing for Novgorod. Venetia Nelms, one of the team members, was unable to sleep that night. She said that she was under an attack of fear but knew that the enemy was attempting to prevent her from praying. She got up to pray and a certain praise and worship song began to rise up in her spirit. The Lord then told her to turn to Psalms 105 and 108. She read Psalm 105:1–15, 39–45. This speaks of God sending individuals, few in number, to the nations; no one was allowed to oppress or touch the prophets. Also, verse 39 speaks of God spreading out a cloud as a covering. The chapter goes on to say that "he gave them the lands of the nations." The Lord then reminded Venetia that she was reading this on October 5 (10/5). She felt that this was God's promise to the team as we began to go into battle. The

Lord then instructed her to turn to Psalm 108. The last two verses of this chapter are the exact words of the worship song the Lord placed in Venetia's spirit when she awoke. Verse 13 states, "With God we will gain the victory, and he will trample down our enemies."

The next evening we had a team meeting and Venetia shared this information. Chris Walden, another team member, grew excited. He said that the Lord had directed him to Psalms 106 and 107 the same night. We realized that all of these numbers, 105, 106, 107 and 108, were the same dates that we were traveling to, praying in and leaving Novgorod (10/5, 10/6, 10/7, 10/8). We knew that we had our marching orders for these four days! While we were in Novgorod, the sky was overcast every time we went into warfare prayer. And after we prayed and had breakthrough, the clouds would break and the sun would appear. The promise from Psalm 105:39!

We arrived in Novgorod, Russia, on October 5 and started praying on October 6.

On this day the Lord provided us with the most informed English-speaking guide in Novgorod, Galina. She was not a believer, but she helped us tremendously. She was impressed with our knowledge of the history of Novgorod and Kiev and the Lord used her to give us key insight. One of the important historical/spiritual facts that she shared with the team was that Novgorod is the father of all Russian history and Kiev is the mother of all Russian history. This was confirmation that we were definitely hitting two very key cities. We had great favor with her.

The people of Novgorod worship St. Sophia and "Our Lady of the Sign." They consider "the lady" the guardian of Novgorod and give her the glory for their survival and growth. The history of this land is steeped in war and battles. After the Nazi invasion during World War II, only 42 original citizens of Novgorod remained alive. There were numerous other bloody battles and wars throughout the history. This is a blatant sign that there is heavy worship of the Queen of

Heaven. It is obvious that all the human sacrifices made to her and Perun were the open door for all this war and trauma. Yet the people of Novgorod give her the glory for their survival.

We prayed at two locations on this day. The most significant was the location called Perun Skete, which is the site where Perun worship occurred one thousand years before Christ! Human sacrifices were performed at this location. The Orthodox Church later built a monastery and a church dedicated to "Our Lady of the Sign" on the burial mound of the children, men and women sacrificed to the pagan god Perun.

When we arrived, a priest gave us the history of the land. He was proud of the fact that Perun was worshiped on this land and that the "Our Lady of the Sign" Church was built on top of the burial mound. He also shared that they want to build a convent there on the land with the intent of making worship of Perun more active in the future!

After our history lesson, we asked if we could walk the grounds alone. The priest and Galina gladly obliged. Before leaving the church, Greg and Darla Ryden blew out the candles that burn in worship to "Our Lady" and Mary. We then began to move in the direction where the sacrifices to Perun took place. As we crossed the field, a low groan began to fill the air and as we got closer to the forest grove, the groan turned into a high-pitched demonic scream. This lasted uninterrupted for one to two minutes. It was humanly impossible to produce that sound.

Everyone on the team heard this except for Greg, who was at the head of the group and totally focused on the site. The closer he got to the grove, the louder the scream became. Needless to say that when we were deep in the grove, we were ready to pray! We broke the power of the blood sacrifices made to Perun and Mokosha; furthermore, we broke their power off the land and the people and asked God to cleanse the land. We anointed one of the keys with oil and buried it along with mustard seeds. We built an altar to the Lord on top of them as we worshiped Him and read Psalm 106, focusing on verses 34–48. We proclaimed that this place would not be given over to a convent and further worship of the Queen of Heaven.

On the way out we prayed around the church, anointed the ground and the door of the church with oil and broke the spirit of death and Antichrist. As we walked to the bus, the priest came outside the monastery and looked at us and then back at the church repeatedly with a perplexed look on his face. He did not see us praying because we were not in view of the monastery. All the team members saw him doing this and felt that he was aware that something had upset the spiritual atmosphere of this place! Save him, Lord!

We had an incredible time on Sunday, October 7. We were without a guide and our bus driver did not speak English, but before Galina left us on Saturday, she asked where we wanted to go and made a map for the bus driver. We knew we would be totally free to pray without any hindrances! Galina gave us a history lesson on all the locations. Once again she confirmed information that we had learned through our research and gave us more key insight into Novgorod. It is considered the "Holiest of Holies" of all Orthodox cities. They have experienced a "great religious revival of Orthodoxy in the past twenty years." She said that the Orthodox are very proud of the fact that there are only four Baptist churches, one Catholic church and one bigger church in addition to the Orthodox churches.

We prayed at several locations on this day. Most of them were Orthodox churches dedicated to Sophia, "Our Lady of the Sign" or some other form of the Queen of Heaven. The two most significant were in St. Sophia's and the Virgin of Mercy. The worship in these places to the Queen of Heaven is very strong and blatant, much like what we saw in Rome.

The Virgin of Mercy, built in the nineteenth century, is the second-most-active church in Novgorod at this time because St. Sophia is venerated above all others. We entered the church during a service and what we saw grieved us greatly. All of the icons and paintings venerated Mary. Jesus was never above her or on His throne. Mary was on the throne, with God and Jesus at her sides crowning her. There was even a picture of Jesus and Mary crowning the Queen of Heaven (Sophia) as she sat on the throne. There was not one place in this church that glorified Jesus. It reminded me so much of Rome. All church members are required to buy candles at each service to light to the saints. They can pay money to get answers to prayer. They believe that the more they pay, the better the prayer coverage and the more powerful answer from God.

After watching, learning, discerning and praying inside, we went outside behind the church and prayed. We wept and asked for forgiveness for these people bound to darkness. We then began to break the power of the Queen of Heaven off this church and asked God to make it a place for His worship; accordingly, we dealt with the Antichrist spirit and cried out for the lost souls gripped in this darkness. We also asked God to visit the priests in dreams and visions so that they will come to the saving knowledge of Jesus Christ. We then worshiped the Lord and sang worship songs to Him. We anointed the key with oil and buried it along with mustard seeds. God's presence on us during this time was precious and incredible.

We then made our way to St. Sophia's. Before going inside, we dealt with another issue that occurred outside the church several hundred years ago. Ivan the Terrible, who was a ruthless, demonically led ruler of Novgorod and Kiev, felt that the people of Novgorod were too free in spirit and were therefore difficult to rule. He arrived in the city for a two-week period and randomly chose men, women and children to be brought by his soldiers to St. Sophia's where they were tortured and killed in the outside courtyard of the church. Galina said, "At this time in history, the floors of the church were stained with blood of hundreds of the slain. Afterward Ivan the Terrible would attend the services in St. Sophia, which were held every day of the week."

In other words, after slaughtering helpless citizens, he would go to the services, repent before the priest, receive forgiveness from the priest, and then go back outside and begin the killings again. This went on for two weeks. Hundreds of people were slaughtered. The sole purpose was to break the free spirit of Novgorod and to gain complete authority over all his subjects. This is reminiscent of Vladimir and the forced baptism. Again this evil happened under the authority of the Queen of Heaven. Obviously we prayed here and broke the spirit of death and control.

Inside the church, we began to investigate and pray. This cathedral houses the wonderworking icon of "Our Lady of the Sign." In centuries past, every time soldiers went into battle they carried this icon in front of the army and prayed continually to her as the battle raged. She is given credit for the victories. In one battle they hung the icon on the fortress walls and an arrow struck "Our Lady" in the eye. She became angry and allowed the defeat of the enemy. Her eye is still out today. This St. Sophia Cathedral was built by Yaroslav the Wise, Vladimir's son. It was built in connection with the St. Sophia Cathedral in Kiev, which was built as the sister church to St. Sophia's in Constantinople. This is obviously a three-strand cord of the enemy.

Greg made a statement in a quiet manner. All the people, especially the women, would bow to the icon, kiss it and cross themselves every time they walked by it. Greg began to walk over to the icon, stand in front of it, stare at it and pray under his breath to God. He never bowed or worshiped her in any manner. Then he would back away and leave enough room for one of the women to step between him and the icon. It upset the old women that he did not pay homage to the icon in the "proper" manner. Instantly they would move in front of the icon, bow to it and cross themselves repeatedly as if to make up for his lack of worship and homage. He did this several times and each time the women would work harder to make up for his "rebellion."

This was not done to upset the women but to point out the extreme fear, bondage and superstition associated with this icon. The bodies of dead saints in coffins lie throughout the cathedral, and they are worshiped and kissed as well. Candles are burning continuously to these dead saints, Sophia and "Our Lady of the Sign." All who come to worship have paid money to buy the candles and the answers to their prayers.

We covered our hands with anointing oil and anointed all the coffins and the icon. I stood in front of the icon and pronounced that her other eye would be destroyed, that she would become totally blind and would no longer be able to find her way in Novgorod. We pronounced her defeat and proclaimed that the people would be blind to her and begin to worship the true and living God. I planted a key covered with oil in a hole in one of the pillars of the temple.

Then we gathered and prayed as a team and in unity pronounced the defeat of this goddess. We broke the spiritual tie between this cathedral and the cathedrals built to St. Sophia in Kiev and Constantinople; we also broke the connection to Greece and the Greek Orthodox Church. In doing this we also dealt with the tie to Roman Catholicism because Greek Orthodoxy and Russian Orthodoxy stem from Roman Catholicism. I then read our scriptural marching orders for the day: Psalm 107. It is amazing how many of the verses in this psalm describe different periods of time in the history of Novgorod! We then asked the Lord to begin to bring a spiritual revival to these people, to cancel the Orthodox religious revival and to bring the people to salvation. We also asked the Lord to bless the work of the few born-again churches in Novgorod so that they would begin to see people come to their services and salvation and deliverance occur.

Our goal in Novgorod was to deal a blow to the darkness that grips this ancient pagan city of Russia. It was obvious that spiritual warfare at this level had never occurred here. We experienced incredible prayer times, but we also could sense that we were the first to war against the demonic foundations of the city at this level. I feel that that we were obedient to our assignment, but it would be great for another team to go into Novgorod and pray again.

Kiev

Upon arriving in Kiev, we met with our contact, Glen West-scott, at the hotel that evening and mapped out the locations where we felt that the Lord was leading us to pray. Glen also brought our Christian interpreter, Yana, who was incredible. I explained to him that we had to find the area of Trypillian culture and the Devich Mount because the Lord told me this was a key location and had confirmed this through some of the intercessors as well. Glen said he would do all he could to find the location.

The Monastery of the Caves was also a strategic location in Kiev. Glen explained that there was an instructor employed at his Bible College who was a saved, Spirit-filled priest who would help us with this site. He was formally a priest in the Orthodox Church and was involved in worship at this site. I was pleased to discover this information.

On October 9, we began to pray in Kiev. We had received many words from the intercessors that we would see great signs in Kiev. This proved to be true. The first location we visited was Babyn Yar where the Nazis killed more than one hundred thousand Jews and Ukrainians during World War II. They lured the people there by telling them that they were taking them to a better and safer place to live. They then took them to a huge ravine, lined them up, shot them and pushed them into the ravine. Whether they were killed by the bullets or not, they were all pushed into the ravine. Dirt and wood were thrown on top of these individuals. The Nazis would then bring the next unfortunate group out and continue the process. Yana explained that the townspeople reported hearing groans from underneath the ground for weeks after the shootings because people were buried alive. The ground literally would move as individuals tried to get out of this grave.

We had a moving time of prayer at this location and four of us on the team with German blood repented for this horrific act of persecution. The Scripture we read was Genesis 4:6–10, which speaks of the blood of Abel crying out to the Lord from the ground. Then we prayed that the bloodshed on this ground would be cleansed and that souls would come into the Kingdom for every drop of blood shed on this land. Patsy Chmelar felt that she was the one to bury the key and mustard seeds at this location. Chad read a Scripture of release and blessing. Patsy then rang out a cry of "Freedom!" There was such an anointing on this proclamation! God continued to use this cry over and over again as we prayed in Kiev.

We prayed at St. Sophia's, which is another cathedral where blatant worship to the Queen of Heaven occurs. They are very strict in this cathedral, but we were actually able to pray inside, gathered in a corner on the second floor. We again severed the ties between the St. Sophia's in Constantinople and Novgorod; furthermore, we pronounced her defeat and proclaimed that Jesus is the Savior and that He is the one who will be worshiped in Kiev. We then found an area where they were repairing some of the tiles and planted a key. We then sang worship songs to the Lord on the way out of the cathedral.

The next stop was the monument of Vladimir where we prayed about the forced baptisms and broke the power of this act off the people and the land. We also broke the lie that he was responsible for the Christianization of Russia and Ukraine because he only brought fear, control and death. It is historical truth that Christianity was already present before Vladimir.

We then made a stop at St. Vladimir's Cathedral, which is a very active church with the Queen of Heaven at the center of worship. Vladimir is depicted as Jesus on a huge mural in the church. If one was uneducated, which the Orthodox believers here generally are, you would think that he was Jesus. The paintings of God looked just like Zeus. People were praying to the dead saints and to Mary.

There was a very demonic-looking female saint painted as an icon on the wall of the cathedral. She had the appearance of death. We asked two nuns and a priest the name of this goddess and they were unable to tell us. They had no clue! We asked a cleaning woman the identity of this goddess. She told us the woman was monarchy, and added, "Monarchy was always mean and stern, thus her appearance."

This woman then asked me if I liked their church. I explained that it was very different from the churches I attended in the United States and that we pray to Jesus, not to Mary. She became intrigued and began to ask many questions about Jesus and the Bible. She told us that she does not read her Bible; she listens to the priests. But she said that her mother tells her that she should read her Bible. She also told me that she prays to Mary because Mary is closer to us. As I shared the Gospel with this woman, we were approached by another woman who began to yell in Russian at our interpreter, Yana. Yana handled her very well, but this woman continued to yell. Yana grabbed me by the arm after five minutes of arguing with this woman and pulled me away. I asked what she was saying. Yana explained that she was accusing us of being from a cult and a false religion and that we were trying to demonically influence her Orthodox sister because praying to Jesus is a cult.

We turned around and the cleaning woman had returned, wanting to know more truth. We shared with her again and asked her if she wanted to know Jesus and ask Him into her heart. She said that she had never heard these truths before and would go home and read her Bible to investigate more. Nan and Patsy gave her a financial blessing from the Lord. She asked if she should give it to the temple and Mary. We told her it was a gift from Jesus to her and that she was not to give it to the temple. We then laid hands on her and prayed for her. Yana invited her to her church. Yana shared that it was extremely unusual for a person of this woman's beliefs to ask questions, and to do so inside the temple was almost unheard of. She said that our prayers were already making a difference to those gripped in darkness. On the way out, we prayed that this woman would get saved and also prayed for the woman who yelled at Yana. This woman did approach Yana before we left the temple and apologized for interrupting our conversation and yelling at us. Yana said that it was also unusual to receive an apology.

The last location where we prayed this day was the Gate Tower, which was the original ancient gate leading into Kiev. When Yaroslav the Wise was ruler, he required all those entering Kiev to pay gold before being granted entrance into the city. We climbed to the top of the tower and instantly felt the Lord stirring us to pray. We began to sing and worship the Lord. We proclaimed that, as this gate tower represented the ancient doorway into the city, the gates of darkness would be shut, and then we invited the King of Glory to come in. Darla Ryden sang prophetically over the city and we then prayed, prophesied and proclaimed the Lord's agenda over Kiev and Ukraine. We all felt impressed to release a cry of freedom again. We stood on the tower overlooking the city and faced north, south, east and west. In unison we exclaimed, "Freedom!" three times over the city. There was an incredible anointing in this proclamation. We felt that every time the Lord had us proclaim this over this territory, spiritual freedom was released over the land. Even though these people are no longer under the reign of Communism, the effects of this oppression are still prevalent. People have a difficult time laughing freely and expressing themselves. It was one of our prayers that freedom would be released over the citizens of Ukraine.

At the hotel that evening, as we waited for dinner, Glen called Greg and me to come down to the lobby. As we approached him he asked, "What have you guys been doing?" He was excited. We stated, "Praying," not knowing where his comment was leading. He explained that he was having difficulty finding the location of the Trypillian culture and the Devich Mount so he asked God to help him. While we were out praying, Vlad, one of the graduate students from the Bible College, came to see Glen and ask for assistance. He explained to Glen that he had read five of Peter Wagner's books on prayer and spiritual warfare and that he needed someone to train him in spiritual warfare prayer. He shared that he lives, pastors and ministers in a region called Trepolie that is difficult to penetrate with the Gospel. Glen stopped him and stated, "Vlad, say the name of the region again." He answered, "Trepolie." This is the Russian word for Trypillian! Vlad shared with Glen that he had written his research paper on this area, its ancient culture and pagan practices! Glen told him that there was a group in Kiev from Global Harvest Ministries under Peter Wagner looking for this location. Vlad and Glen were so excited. Glen was like a schoolboy. Vlad knew all the locations where we wanted to pray and could take us there. This became the agenda for the next day.

Glen also shared that Sergei, the Spirit-filled priest in the Reformed Orthodox movement, was able to meet with us on Thursday at the Monastery of the Caves, the Lavra. Glen said that this would be a very important meeting. He talked with us about the underground tunnels that are 180 miles long and connect the monastery with one of the most demonic regions of Ukraine. Sergei would be able to give us crucial insight into Orthodoxy and direction as to how to pray. The agenda was then set for Thursday. That evening after dinner, we had a group meeting and prayer time. I told the team that we were about to hit the major strongholds of this region and to be prepared. We called GHM and all our intercessors and mobilized them to pray. We were going into the enemy's camp!

On Wednesday, we awoke ready to go to Tripoli. We started off the day on a tour of a museum in this region. We gathered more insight and information, including the fact that the Slavic tribes worshiped the eagle and deer. I explained to the team that I felt the Lord directing us to pray in all the small villages that were in the region or under the influence of this Devich Mount and, at the end of the day, we would climb the mount and pray. We then made our way to a town called Vytachiv. This is the town that the New Age occult group, the Ukrainian Spiritual Republic, calls the road to enlightenment. I was getting very excited! By the way, there are no churches or Orthodox temples in this village.

We drove to the edge of a village and came upon a windmill, a small wooden temple and three cornerstones all dedicated to the Queen of Heaven. I could not believe my eyes! I knew that the Ukrainian Spiritual Republic worshiped here, but to see monuments, cornerstones and temples was a total surprise. We swarmed the place. Many of us instantly ran to the cornerstones, which were blatantly dedicated to the Queen of Heaven. They had her picture and writings dedicating this land to the Great Moist Mother Earth. There was also a "ying and yang" symbol on the middle stone. On the last stone there was a picture of an eagle's body with outstretched wings with the face of the Queen of Heaven. Greg, Chad and Chris ran to the wooden temple and tried to get in, but it was locked. Then they built a human ladder with Chad on bottom and Chris on top. Chris was able to see into the temple, which, of course, had pictures of the Queen of Heaven. There was a strange cross on top of the temple, which we also discovered at the entrance of the Lavra the next day. Jonathan went to check out the windmill, which also had the Queen of Heaven stationed at the entrance. This location and the Devich Mount are situated on the Dnieper River. There was something in the rivers and waterways, but the Lord has not revealed all the pieces to this part of the puzzle as of yet.

About this time a car drove up. It was the mayor of the city. He explained that he had the key to the temple and the windmill and that he would let us in! Not only did he allow us into the temple and the windmill, but he also gave us total privacy. Oh, boy, did we pray! Of course, Yana and her husband were busy talking with him and distracting him as well. Inside the temple were items dedicated to the worship of the Queen of Heaven and Kupala. It did have a picture of Jesus, which was strange because Berdnyk feels that he has uncovered the secrets of Christ and has written a book called *Christ's Secrets*.

On the wall was a friendship/spiritual covenant between this occult group and the village sealed with an emblem with an image of the Queen of Heaven! The date that this covenant was signed was 1992. We got very excited! This was the same year that Glen and Natasha began their work in Kiev with St. James Bible College. The vision of this school is to train up Spirit-filled leaders in Ukraine who will flow in the anointing of the Lord and carry the spiritual tools necessary to see this area of the world reached with the Gospel. They are training the future apostles, prophets, teachers, evangelists, pastors and intercessors. They bring in Christian leaders from around the world to train the students for two-week periods.

I felt the spirit of prophecy and began to prophesy to Glen: "The date on this covenant is a prophetic statement about your call to and work in Kiev. The enemy was establishing the counterfeit at the same time the Lord was establishing His work for the future generations of Kiev and Ukraine. God is revealing to you, Glen, this day the schemes of the enemy so that you and your leaders can begin to do effective, targeted spiritual warfare prayer over Kiev and Ukraine, to prevent future generations from being gripped by darkness but brought into the Kingdom purposes for their lives and the nation. God will give you the tools to deal with this plan of the enemy, and as you pray the righteous leadership of Kiev will be brought to the forefront and the false leadership will diminish. These tools and insight will also give you strategies to pray for breakthrough in the Orthodox Church. God is also raising you up to be a key leader in Kiev." Glen was so overcome that he was shaking. He was speechless. Then Venetia gave him $180 as a sign of a breakthrough in finances and a sowing into the move of God into Ukraine. It was really awesome.

Of course, we did spiritual warfare prayer and began to break the power of the Queen of Heaven off this area. Glen prayed and broke the power of this covenant and pronounced the move of the Holy Spirit into this region. We anointed the seal and all the icons with oil and broke their power. Mary's picture was falling in the frame, so we pronounced that her worship would completely fall and this group would no longer worship her, but the true and living God. We then headed for the windmill to join the other half of the team.

Jonathan and Greg looked right at me and said, "You really want to go inside the windmill." I gladly obliged. When we got inside I could not believe it. This was the temple and sanctuary of the occult group leader, Berdnyk! In it he had pictures of the three temples that they want to build. It had a picture of Buddha and the Queen of Heaven. It also had the same friendship/spiritual covenant with the seal of the Queen of Heaven. A filing cabinet contained all the books that this man had written about the Queen of Heaven and his New Age beliefs. On one of the walls was his vision statement. It was written in Russian. I cannot remember it word for word, but it talked of walking in peace as a child or taking up a sword and walking as a warrior. I felt a very strong warning from the Lord. I told Glen that if this group was not dealt with in the spiritual realm, that it had the potential of becoming a very dangerous cult that would eventually cause bloodshed. Jonathan said that he had the same impression. We prayed and broke the power of bloodshed and asked God to break these people out of their deception and bring them to salvation.

We formed a circle around the three cornerstones dedicated to the Queen of Heaven, held hands and worshiped the Lord. The Lord's presence was so precious and awesome. We broke the power of the Queen of Heaven over these stones and pronounced that there would never be three temples built to her. We then formed a tight group in front of the cornerstones and Vlad buried one of the keys covered in oil along with mustard seeds behind the middle cornerstone. We hid him because the mayor was watching us at this point. He did not speak English and thought we were worshiping the goddess. Oh, well! Leaving the town we stopped by the mayor's home per his request, and he gave us a book about the village and the occult group as a memento. Isn't God good!

Afterward on the bus we were looking through our research and realized that in one of the pictures of Berdnyk, the leader of this cult was holding an ax. One of the villages in this Devich Mount region was overcome by an ax murderer who brutally killed hundreds of villagers. There are also spiritual myths about the ax, and it was revered and worshiped in ancient days. No wonder we had the warning from the Lord!

We made our way to the heart of five villages in this region that formed a circle with the Devich Mount being at the head of the circle. We would pray at the center of these villages and break the power of the worship to the Queen of Heaven and her hold on the Orthodox Church. This region is one of the most difficult to penetrate with the Gospel. Vlad shared that there is an Orthodox priest in this region who holds great power over the people. Vlad will gather pastors and come to a region, fast and pray, then begin to evangelize. He will hold meetings and people will get saved. The priest will hear about it and come to the village and frighten the people and tell them they are part of a cult and that they are bound to hell. He scares and threatens them and then takes all their money to "help secure their place in heaven again." These villagers become so frightened that they will not attend another meeting.

We prayed in this priest's village and broke his territorial control over this region, and we also prayed in the village of the first woman saved and delivered in this region. She and her husband partner with Vlad and lead prayer meetings in their home in an attempt to reach the village. Vlad and Glen took us to their home where we prayed and asked God to bless their work and that it will prosper. We prayed a blessing over this couple and their family and then gave them a financial blessing to sow into the new thing God is doing. Then the woman insisted on blessing us. She gave us curdled sour milk to drink! Glen looked at me and said, "Be very brave." Due to the fact that we did not want to insult this family, we all took a sip and passed the cup on to the next person. It was terrible! Of course, we did not let this couple know that we were not enjoying it. Yana's husband, Eugene, and Vlad love this milk, so they rescued us and drank all of it. Thank You, Lord, for small answers to prayer! In all of these villages, we decreed a cry of freedom, which Glen taught us in Russian, "Svaboda! Svaboda! Svaboda!"

After praying in these five villages we went to the Mount and climbed to the top. It is very old. Many of the ancient relics associated with the worship of the Queen of Heaven have been excavated. This mount is also a huge burial mound of the ancient people involved with worshiping Great Mother Earth and those sacrificed to her. It is a huge graveyard. The Ukrainian Spiritual Republic group comes here for yearly holidays and festivals, but the members also come here to pray on a daily basis.

Two women from the village below came to the top of the mount to speak with us. They told us boldly that they were Christians and asked, "Are you Christians or members of the Ukrainian Spiritual Republic?" We told them we were Christians. They showed us the location where the Ukrainian Spiritual Republic had recently climbed the mount, buried a time capsule and drawn a star in the ground to show the burial site. They then left us.

The star was a six-pointed star in the shape of the Star of David. The meaning of this star was originally attached to witchcraft and magic. The significance of the double triangle means diverse things in different cultures. In Hebrew, for instance, it expresses the way one dimension pours itself into the next dimension. It is a sacred process and sacred path. A very interesting fact about this star is the attachment to Vladimir. Before the forced baptisms, Vladimir built a sanctuary to the gods Perun, Dazhbog, Chors, Simargl, Stribog and the goddess Mokosha. On the outside of this sanctuary he had these gods and goddesses positioned in the form of this star. Also the gods and goddesses Volos, Zeus, Divanna and Kupala were worshiped here. I believe that this star was drawn here by this New Age group as a sign representing the spiritual connection of the worship of the Queen of Heaven to past, present and future generations. They desire to perpetuate her worship and reclaim Ukraine for her glory.

We prayed for about an hour on this mount. We repented for the ancient people and their pagan practices. We then began to break the tie between the goddesses and the gods. We broke the power of the Antichrist spirit, the spirit of death, fear, witchcraft, control and perversion. We read Scripture and worshiped the Lord. Glen, Vlad, Yana and Eugene sang the Ukrainian Communion song about the blood of Jesus. The anointing was incredible! We laid hands on all four of these Ukrainians and asked God to bless their work, to further the Gospel and His purposes in Kiev through them. The group broke out in praise to the Lord and thanked Him for His goodness and His promises and decreed Kiev to awake and arise. Then facing outward to the north, south, east and west, we proclaimed freedom: "Svabota, Svabota, Svabota!" Nine keys covered with oil were planted with mustard seeds in the ground right next to the time capsule. Glen and Vlad were going to return that weekend with a shovel to bury two Bibles, one written in Russian and the other in Ukrainian. They would also try to dig up the time capsule to see the contents and then destroy it. This might prove to be difficult because the Ukrainian Spiritual Republic covered the capsule with cement. In spite of this, they were still going to try. What a powerful day! God is good!

I knew that the day of praying at the Monastery of the Caves, the Lavra, was going to be eye-opening. In our first team meeting six months before, the Lord gave me a word that He was going to take us to an underground cemetery dedicated to the Queen of Heaven, which was a key location to the spiritual breakthrough of Kiev. In our research we discovered the Monastery of the Caves founded in the year A.D. 1051. It houses the Near and Far Caves, which contain the bones of 120 dead saints, priests, famous artists and doctors. This monastery is huge and is considered the most sacred and important location of Orthodoxy in Ukraine. I was up interceding the whole night before going to this location. I knew God was going to reveal something incredible.

We arrived at 10:00 A.M. and waited for Sergei, the Spirit-filled priest involved in the Reformed Orthodox Church. This was a divine appointment from God with this incredible man. He told us that he had to give us the history and information before entering the monastery because the priests do not like him. He explained that there is a religious mafia in the Orthodox Church that torments those who have experienced the Lord and become saved. Many people marvel at the fact that he is still alive. He would try to go in with us, but if he was recognized he would have to leave immediately or there would be trouble. He said to be prepared for anything when entering. Glen later told us that Sergei lives every day knowing that his life and the lives of his wife and five daughters are in grave danger.

In the history lesson he shared with us keys to seeing the worship of the Queen of Heaven in the Orthodox Church brought down. He told us that in the 5th and 6th centuries paganism began to infiltrate the Church in a major way. It was already there but grew very strong at this point. The monarchy began to gain forced power in the Church, and they wanted to bring their pagan practices and political corruption into the Church and mingle it with the worship. We received the full story of Vladimir and the fact that this man had no conversion experience. We were told about the deaths and about the people in Novgorod who were killed and thrown into the Volga River. Citizens of Kiev were killed as well, but once a few people were killed, the rest of the citizens decided to become baptized in order to live and not die.

We learned that the Lavra is the daughter monastery of two monasteries in Greece. The monastery for priests is located on the Aphon Mountain and the other is a convent, but we were not given its exact location. Glen is contacting Sergei for us to find out these exact locations so we can send teams there to pray.

He explained how all services are conducted in the old Slavonic language and it is illegal to conduct a service in Russian. A couple of years ago a test was given to one hundred people who had been in Orthodoxy their entire lives. They were asked to write the interpretation of a prayer. Out of one hundred individuals, only one person was able to interpret the prayer and even that person did not get much of the interpretation correct. Even the priests do not know and understand everything they are saying and praying. If priests preach or speak the services in Russian, they will be excommunicated. They teach, preach and pray false teaching all the time and the people are clueless. The love of money is strong, but the priests and monks are extremely lazy and do not want to do any work. This laziness of the priests and monks affects the cities and nations in which they are located. It causes laziness in the people of these countries. The priests and monks are the first and most powerful ones to come against the move of the Spirit and the reformation that is occurring in the Orthodox Church. There are a few priests who have had an encounter with Jesus and will dress in civilian clothes and come to Sergei's church to hear the Word of God. Unfortunately many of these men are afraid to leave the Church for fear they will be harmed or killed.

Sergei told us that there used to be a convent connected to the monastery by underground tunnels, but the convent was moved because a burial ground was discovered behind the convent with dead and aborted babies. The priests were the ones who fathered these children. Homosexuality is a major issue among the priests. Some repent of this, but not many. Many of them are alcoholics and drug addicts. Sergei led several priests and monks to the Lord and has brought them through deliverance. He is praying for more to be set free. In his church, he has a map of Ukraine hanging on a wall. They have placed a red flag on the map in each location of an Orthodox church, monastery or convent that he considers to carry the most significant spiritual weight. He and his church members pray over this map daily, believing God for breakthrough. They have been praying for God to bring other people from other nations to pray with them for breakthrough. We were the firstfruits of these prayers and he began to thank God for us. Needless to say, many of us began to weep. He laid hands on us and prayed for us and then we laid hands on him and prayed for him. It was a precious time.

I asked him the most important location to pray in the monastery to break the powers that control this region. He instantly answered, "The caves." People come from all around to worship the dead bones of these 120 people, which are considered to be the wonderworking icons of Ukraine. He told us the spirits to pray against are corruption, greed, perversion, homosexuality, death, fear, control, political corruption, witchcraft and Antichrist. Breaking occult practices and the worship of the Queen of Heaven is obviously a key strategy. We then entered the monastery.

While walking down the walkway, we heard a policeman yelling at us in Russian. We thought we were in trouble because we had Sergei with us. This was not the case. We moved to the sidewalk and coming down the walkway behind us was a huge procession. Sergei had forgotten that it was October 11, the day of the Feast of the Bones! This is the day when the priests, monks, nuns and Orthodox followers go down into the caves and worship the bones. God was taking us in on the feast day!

As the procession began the priests at the front were carrying an icon of Mary and they sang a song that sounded like a funeral dirge. Sergei and Yana explained that they were singing to Mary and the dead saints. The procession lasted about twenty minutes as about five hundred participants made their way to the caves. This was a sad moment for Sergei because he used to participate in these occult practices. I asked, "Do you consider Orthodoxy a cult?"

He answered, "Yes."

We waited about five minutes and followed behind the procession. Sergei stopped to give us a little more history of the caves, but a car with three priests pulled up behind him and stopped. They recognized him, but his back was to the car and he did not realize they were there. The priests were about to exit the car and come at him when Greg told Sergei what was occurring behind him. We told him to leave so he would not be in danger. He hugged us and shook our hands and looked at me and said, "You will hit the mark. You will hit the target today." He then left. The priests were satisfied and drove away.

We made our way to the caves. The women in our group put scarves on our heads and we covered our hands with anointing oil. We were going in to pray and break the power of these dead saints and the Queen of Heaven. It took about one hour and thirty minutes to get in because we were at the end of the line. The entire time we waited to get in, these people sang nonstop. Yana explained to us that they sang to Mary and the dead saints and not one time did they ever mention God, Jesus or the Holy Spirit. It was as if they were entranced while they sang. There was no life and you could feel the oppression and heaviness.

We finally got through the doors and got our candles, which we needed to see. Many of the worshipers leave their candles inside to give more power to the prayers of the dead saints.

I told the team that I was praying that our hands would not catch on fire because they were drenched with anointing oil. We began our descent into the extremely overcrowded caves. A priest instantly confronted Yana and accused us of not being there to pray. Yana responded that that was our exact reason for being there! Then a woman in front of her began to fuss because I was wearing lipstick, so I wiped it off. They fussed because Greg had gum so he took it out of his mouth. Yana then grabbed us and said, "Let's go," and we pushed our way into the tunnel.

The tunnel was three feet wide and there were niches that contained coffins of the dead saints. The coffins had glass covers and the bodies were covered with ornate garments. The people sang to the dead bodies and they leaned over and kissed the glass covers. Yana said that there have been stories of the dead bones emitting oil and people being healed as a result. Sergei had also told us that many priests try to live in the caves with the dead bones! Many only live ten to twelve years in that situation, but there was one priest who lived in the caves without ever coming outside for 37 years before dying. How horrific!

We began to lay hands on the coffins and anoint them with oil and announce their defeat. Yana would slip us into niches that had altars to Mary or a dead saint and say, "Pray here, it is very significant." There was an old woman in front of us with a toddler around the age of eighteen months who was sick. Again and again she took him and laid him on a coffin facedown, as if causing him to kiss the dead saint. He was perfectly quiet until his lips touched the coffin and then he would let out a shriek. It was terrible! Greg, Yana and I were the closest to this and the only ones who could see what was happening. We were crying over the child and furious with the enemy at the same time. Everything took place very quickly because the priest wanted us to leave. We prayed for about ten to fifteen minutes before we came out of the caves. We then went directly above the caves and went into warfare prayer.

We dealt with these occult practices and the worship of the Queen of Heaven. We prayed against all the strongholds that Sergei told us about. We read Psalm 111, prayed over many issues and pronounced that the worship to the Queen of Heaven would be coming down and her defeat was on the way. We asked God to visit the priests, monks and nuns in dreams and visions that they would have a true experience with Jesus. We also broke the tie between Communism and the Russian Orthodox Church. At this writing the Orthodox Church is trying to partner with the government and Communism to rid Russia and Ukraine of all religions but Orthodoxy; we broke this scheme and prayed that all people involved with this will be exposed. Next we prayed against Vladimir and the lie that he was the father of Christianity in Russia. Lastly we broke our candles as a prophetic sign that the prayers to and worship of the dead saints were broken. We then walked out singing, "Went to the enemy's camp and took back what he stole from Kiev." As we walked out the entrance to the monastery, we laid the broken candles on the ground and crushed them as a sign that these dead saints and the Queen of Heaven are being dethroned and defeated. Then we shouted as loud as we could, "Jesus Christ!"

That night I spoke at a church by the name of Grace and Love of Christ Church. We met this group through Derrick at Gideon's Army II. The worship service was incredible. It was wonderful to be in the presence of the Lord after being exposed to all the darkness. The pastor of the church is a woman named Olga Pyrozhenko. She was good friends with Sergei. She asked me to share about our research and all that we did. Olga and the church members were excited over all that was shared because they had been trying to find out about the Trypillian culture to deal with the region in Tripoli, but they had a difficult time locating all the information. They prayed in agreement that as a result of our prayers these villagers will come to salvation. They were awed by the fact that we were able to get into the Lavra on the day of the Feast of the Bones and do warfare. After I spoke, Olga gave an altar call and one young man came forward to be saved. We were so blessed and asked the Lord that this salvation will be the firstfruit of all of our prayers. Olga asked if I would come back and teach at their prophetic conference in the spring. She wants me to teach on prophetic acts in spiritual warfare. I told her I would love to come back if and when the Lord opens the door.

Our goal was to pray over the strongest spiritual issues in Kiev and deal a major blow to them, which I felt we did. We did deal a blow to the Lavra, but it is not completely dealt with. Marty stated that she feels that praying at the monasteries in Greece that are considered the mother and father of the Lavra—the Lavra and Mount Olympus—simultaneously will deal a huge blow to the darkness in the Orthodox Church. Glen is contacting Sergei for us, so we can investigate the strongest points of Orthodoxy in Greece and the location of these two monasteries. I have Sergei's information, but he speaks very little English. Glen will be able to communicate more effectively with him.

This trip was incredible. God was so good. He literally revealed the strongest spiritual issues to pray over and against. It was a privilege to take this team and an honor to be used at this level. I am excited about the next trip. I am already praying and seeking the Lord about the next assignment. Thank you for this opportunity. It was awesome!

Notes

Chapter 1: Explanation of Spiritual Warfare

1. C. Peter Wagner, *What the Bible Says about Spiritual Warfare* (Ventura, Calif.: Regal Books, 2002), 18–19.

Chapter 2: The Earth Is the Lord's

1. George Otis Jr., *The Last of the Giants* (Tarrytown, N.Y.: Chosen Books, 1991), 88.

2. Hector P. Torres, *Pulling Down Strongholds* (Colorado Springs: Wagner Institute for Practical Ministry, 1999), 184.

3. Alistair Petrie, *Releasing Heaven on Earth* (Grand Rapids, Mich.: Chosen Books, 2000), 22.

4. Pacific Christian Ministries, *The Conquest of Canaan*, www.pacmin.com/museum/canaan.shtml.

5. David B. Guralnik, ed., *Webster's New World Dictionary* (New York: Simon and Schuster, 1982), 326.

6. C. Peter Wagner, *Confronting the Queen of Heaven* (Colorado Springs: Wagner Publications, 1998), 24.

7. See the "Catechism of the Catholic Church," Part One, Section Two, Chapter Three, Article Nine; www.vatican.va.

8. See the "Catechism of the Catholic Church," Part One, Section Two, Chapter Two, Article Three; www.vatican.va.

9. www.vatican.va (30 April 2000).

10. Harold Harman, "The Kinship of the Virgin Mary: Profile of a Cultural Archetype," *Revision Magazine*, 1998, 4. (This article can be found on eLibrary.)

11. Ibid.
12. Peter De Rosa, *Vicars of Christ: The Dark Side of the Papacy* (New York: Crown, 1988), 5.
13. "History of the Basilica," http:/it-jabba-stuweb.coloradocollege.edu/_larson/History_of_the_Basilica.html.
14. Watchman Nee, *Changed into His Likeness* (Wheaton, Ill.: Tyndale House, 1978), 28–29.

Chapter 3: Revelation of Assignment

1. Wagner, *Spiritual Warfare*, 11.

Chapter 4: Team Dynamics

1. Chuck D. Pierce and John Dickson, *Worship Warrior* (Ventura, Calif.: Regal Books, 2002), 110.
2. Ibid., 114–115.

Chapter 5: Exposing Hidden Truths

1. Cindy Tosto, *Taking Possession of the Land* (Colorado Springs: Wagner Publications, 2001), 44.
2. Moses W. Redding, *The Illustrated History of Freemasonry* (New York: Redding & Co., 1901), 56–57.

Chapter 6: Spiritual Mapping

1. George Otis Jr., *Informed Intercession* (Ventura, Calif.: Renew Books, 1999), 85.
2. Quoted in Otis, *The Last of the Giants*, 84.
3. Defined by Alice Smith in a teaching entitled "Spiritual Warfare/Mapping."
4. Otis, *The Last of the Giants*, 88.
5. *Encarta World Dictionary*, North American Edition, www.onelook.com.
6. *Webster's 1828 Dictionary*, Electronic Version by Christian Technologies, Inc., www.onelook.com.
7. David Taylor, "Putting Things Straight (Introducing Earth Mysteries)," www.whitedragon.org.uk (1994).
8. *Encarta World Dictionary*, North American Edition, www.onelook.com.
9. Smith, "Spiritual Warfare/Mapping."
10. Robert Todd Carroll, "Ley Lines," in *The Skeptic's Dictionary* (Hoboken, N.J.: John Wiley and Sons, 2002), www.skepdic.com/leylines.html.

Chapter 7: Preparing for Battle

1. Barbara Wentroble, *Prophetic Intercession* (Ventura, Calif.: Regal Books, 1999), 48.

Chapter 8: Advancing into Battle

1. Wentroble, *Prophetic Intercession*, 113.
2. John Dawson, *Taking Our Cities for God* (Lake Mary, Fla.: Creation House, 1989), 39.

Chapter 9: Counterattack

1. Wentroble, *Prophetic Intercession*, 170.

Chapter 10: Breakthrough!

1. Barbara Yoder, *The Breaker Anointing* (Colorado Springs: Wagner Publications, 2001), 12–13.

Bibliography

Alves, Elizabeth. *Becoming a Prayer Warrior*. Ventura, Calif.: Regal Books, 1998.

Arnold, Clinton E. *Ephesians: Power and Magic*. Grand Rapids, Mich.: Baker Book House, 1992.

———. *Powers of Darkness*. Downers Grove, Ill.: InterVarsity Press, 1992.

Collins, Mary Ann. *Freedom from Catholicism*. Colorado Springs, Colo.: Wagner Publications, 2001.

———. *Unmasking Catholicism*. Lincoln, Neb.: iUniverse, Inc., 2003.

Connor, Kevin J. *Interpreting the Symbols and Types*. Portland, Ore.: Bible Temple Publishing, 1992.

Damazio, Frank. *The Making of a Leader*. Portland, Ore.: Trilogy Productions, 1988.

De Rosa, Peter. *Vicars of Christ: The Dark Side of the Papacy*. New York: Crown Publishers, 1988.

Deere, Jack. *Surprised by the Voice of God*. Grand Rapids, Mich.: Zondervan, 1996.

Grubb, Norman. *Rees Howells, Intercessor*. Fort Washington, Pa.: Christian Literature Crusade, 1952.

Haggard, Ted. *Primary Purpose*. Lake Mary, Fla.: Creation House, 1995.

―――. *Taking It to the Streets*. Colorado Springs, Colo.: Wagner Publications, 2002.

Hawthorne, Steve and Graham Kendrick. *Prayerwalking*. Lake Mary, Fla.: Creation House, 1993.

Hinn, Benny. *Good Morning, Holy Spirit*. Nashville: Thomas Nelson, 1990.

Jacobs, Cindy. *Possessing the Gates of the Enemy*. Grand Rapids, Mich.: Chosen Books, 1991.

―――. *Deliver Us from Evil*. Ventura, Calif.: Regal Books, 2001.

―――. *The Voice of God*. Ventura, Calif.: Regal Books, 1995.

Kinnaman, Gary. *Overcoming the Dominion of Darkness*. Grand Rapids, Mich.: Chosen Books, 1990.

Michaelsen, Joanna. *The Beautiful Side of Evil*. Eugene, Ore.: Harvest House, 1982.

―――. *Like Lambs to the Slaughter*. Eugene, Ore.: Harvest House, 1989.

Milligan, Ira. *Every Dreamer's Handbook*. Shippensburg, Pa.: Treasure House, 2000.

―――. *Understanding the Dreams You Dream*. Shippensburg, Pa.: Treasure House, 1997.

Murphy, Ed. *The Handbook for Spiritual Warfare*. Nashville: Thomas Nelson, 1992.

Nee, Watchman. *Spiritual Authority*. Richmond, Va.: Christian Fellowship Publisher, 1972.

―――. *Changed into His Likeness*. Wheaton, Ill.: Tyndale House, 1978.

Otis, George Jr. *Informed Intercession*. Ventura, Calif.: Renew Books, 1999.

―――. *The Last of the Giants*. Tarrytown, N.Y.: Chosen Books, 1991.

―――*The Twilight Labyrinth*. Grand Rapids, Mich.: Chosen Books, 1997.

Peretti, Frank E. *This Present Darkness*. Westchester, Ill.: Crossway Books, 1986.

―――. *Piercing the Darkness*. Westchester, Ill.: Crossway Books, 1987.

Petrie, Alistair. *Releasing Heaven on Earth*. Grand Rapids, Mich.: Chosen Books, 2000.

Pierce, Chuck and Rebecca Sytsema. *Ridding Your Home of Spiritual Darkness.* Colorado Springs, Colo.: Wagner Publications, 1999.

———. *Future War of the Church.* Ventura, Calif.: Regal Books, 2001.

———. *When God Speaks.* Colorado Springs, Colo.: Wagner Publications, 2003.

Pierce, Chuck and John Dickson. *Worship Warrior.* Ventura, Calif.: Regal Books, 2002.

Pike, Albert. *Morals and Dogma.* New York: H. Macoy, 1878.

Prince, Derek. *They Shall Expel Demons.* Grand Rapids, Mich.: Chosen Books, 1998.

Redding, Moses W. *The Illustrated History of Freemasonry.* New York: Redding & Co, 1901.

Sheets, Dutch. *Intercessory Prayer.* Ventura, Calif.: Regal Books, 1996.

Sherrer, Quinn and Ruthanne Garlock. *A Woman's Guide to Breaking Bondages.* Ann Arbor, Mich.: Servant Publications, 1994.

———. *The Spiritual Warrior's Prayer Guide.* Ann Arbor, Mich.: Servant Publications, 1992.

Silvoso, Ed. *That None Should Perish.* Ventura, Calif.: Regal Books, 1994.

Sjoberg, Kjell. *Winning the Prayer War.* Chichester, England: New Wine Press, 1991.

Smith, Alice. *Beyond the Veil.* Ventura, Calif.: Regal Books, 1996.

———. *40 Days Beyond the Veil.* Ventura, Calif.: Regal Books, 2003.

———. *Discerning the Climate of the City.* Houston, Tex.: SpiriTruth Publishing, 1997.

———. *Dispelling the Darkness.* Houston, Tex.: SpiriTruth Publishing, 1998.

Smith, Eddie and Alice Smith. *Spiritual Housecleaning.* Ventura, Calif.: Regal Books, 2003.

Smith, Eddie. *Intercessors, How to Understand and Unleash Them for God's Glory.* Houston, Tex.: SpiriTruth Publishing, 1998.

Sorge, Bob. *Envy: The Enemy Within.* Ventura, Calif.: Regal Books, 2003.

Wagner, Doris. *How to Cast Out Demons.* Ventura, Calif.: Regal Books, 2000.

Wagner, C. Peter. *Breaking Strongholds in Your City*. Ventura, Calif.: Regal Books, 1993.

————. *Churches That Pray*. Ventura, Calif.: Regal Books, 1993.

————. *Confronting the Powers*. Ventura, Calif.: Regal Books, 1996.

————. *Discover Your Spiritual Gifts*. Ventura, Calif.: Regal Books, 2002.

————. *Engaging the Enemy*. Ventura, Calif.: Regal Books, 1991.

————. *Humility*. Ventura, Calif.: Regal Books, 2002.

————. *Lighting the World*. Ventura, Calif.: Regal Books, 1995.

————. *Prayer Shield*. Ventura, Calif.: Regal Books, 1992.

————. *Praying with Power*. Ventura, Calif.: Regal Books, 1997.

————. *Warfare Prayer*. Ventura, Calif.: Regal Books, 1992.

————. *What the Bible Says about Spiritual Warfare*. Ventura, Calif.: Regal Books, 2001.

————. *Your Spiritual Gifts Can Help Your Church Grow*. Ventura, Calif.: Regal Books, 1992.

————. *Confronting the Queen of Heaven*. Colorado Springs, Colo.: Wagner Publications, 1998.

————. *Hard Core Idolatry*. Colorado Springs, Colo.: Wagner Publications, 1999.

————. *The Queen's Domain*. Colorado Springs, Colo.: Wagner Publications, 2000.

Wentroble, Barbara. *God's Purpose for Your Life*. Ventura, Calif.: Regal Books, 2002.

————. *Praying with Authority*. Ventura, Calif.: Regal Books, 2003.

————. *Prophetic Intercession*. Ventura, Calif.: Regal Books, 1999.

Yoder, Barbara J. *Mantled with Authority*. Colorado Springs, Colo.: Wagner Publications, 2003.

————. *The Breaker Anointing*. Colorado Springs, Colo.: Wagner Publications, 2001.

Index

Index

Rebecca Greenwood serves as a minister to the Body of Christ. Over the past thirteen years, she has participated in and led spiritual warfare prayer journeys to many cities across the state of Texas and to countries such as Egypt, Nepal, Italy, Turkey, Russia, Ukraine, Ireland and Spain.

She and her husband, Greg, served for five years with Eddie and Alice Smith at the U.S. Prayer Center. During this time, she served as prayer coordinator of Houston House of Prayer and the U.S. Prayer Center, where she led prayer meetings and initiatives, the deliverance ministry and ministry teams. She has also contributed to articles about prayer for *Charisma* and *Pray!* magazine and appeared on TBN representing the *PrayUSA!* initiative.

Rebecca received a degree in vocal performance from Texas Women's University in Denton, Texas, and a diploma in practical ministry from Wagner Leadership Institute in Colorado Springs, Colorado.

Rebecca is currently serving as executive assistant to Peter and Doris Wagner of Global Harvest Ministries in Colorado Springs. She is a member of ISDM (International Society of Deliverance Ministers) under the direction of Peter and Doris Wagner. She also serves as an Eagle of God under the direction of Chuck Pierce of Glory of Zion Ministries International.

Rebecca is founder and president of Christian Harvest International, an international ministry called to equip and disciple the Body of Christ in prayer, spiritual warfare and deliverance. Christian Harvest International also serves as an equipping ministry for those called to strategic-level spiritual warfare with a desire to see the Lord usher in spiritual transformation and revival to the nations and people of the earth.

Rebecca and Greg, dean of Wagner Leadership Institute, reside in Colorado Springs. They have three beautiful daughters, Kendall, Rebecca and Katie.

To contact Rebecca Greenwood or for more information about Christian Harvest International, please contact:

Christian Harvest International
P. O. Box 63150
Colorado Springs, CO 80962-3150
info@christianharvestintl.org
www.christianharvestintl.org